The Winter Queen

THE WINTER QUEEN

The Story of Elizabeth Stuart

JOSEPHINE ROSS

WEIDENFELD AND NICOLSON
London

149

5.8T L

ISBN 0 297 77603 7

Printed in Great Britain by
Willmer Brothers Limited Rock Ferry Merseyside

CONTENTS

List of illustrations   page *vii*

Acknowledgements   *ix*

1 Winter Season   1

3 The Marriage of Thames and Rhine   30

2 Promised Land   9

4 The Electress   49

5 The Queen   68

6 The Distressed Lady   89

7 Family Fortunes   111

8 Eclipse and Glory   142

Index   159

ILLUSTRATIONS

Between pages 118 and 119

James I (National Portrait Gallery)

Anne of Denmark (National Portrait Gallery)

Elizabeth as a child (in the collections of Leeds City Art Galleries)

Henry, Prince of Wales (National Portrait Gallery)

Charles I as Duke of York (Scottish National Portrait Gallery)

Combe Abbey, Warwickshire (Mary Evans Picture Library)

Visscher's Long View of London (by courtesy of the trustees of the British Museum)

Frederick of Bohemia (National Portrait Gallery)

Arrival of Frederick with Elizabeth at Flushing in May 1613, a detail (Frans Halsmuseum Haarlem)

Heidelberg in the early seventeenth century (Mary Evans Picture Library)

The Elector Frederick on the Wheel of Fortune (Mansell Collection)

Prague in 1649 (Mansell Collection)

Charles Louis (by kind permission of His Grace the Duke of Norfolk C.B.; photo by Courtauld Institute of Art)

Prince Rupert (National Gallery London, on loan to the National Portrait Gallery)

Princess Sophia (National Portrait Gallery)

Earl of Craven (National Portrait Gallery)

The Hague in the mid-seventeenth century (Mansell Collection)

Elizabeth (National Gallery London, on loan to the National Portrait Gallery)

ACKNOWLEDGEMENTS

For their help and encouragement while this book was in preparation I am indebted to Christopher Falkus; Gila Falkus; Beatrix Miller; Sir Oliver Millar, Surveyor of the Queen's Pictures, and Mrs Cousland, both of whom gave me valuable advice about the portraiture of the Winter Queen; Dr McKay of the LSE who read and improved the manuscript; Paula Iley who edited it; Jane Thompson who did the picture research; the staffs of the British Museum, the Public Record Office and the London Library; and my husband James.

CHAPTER ONE
Winter Season

When the elderly Queen of Bohemia died in London at Leicester House, on 13 February 1662, there was no display of public emotion such as had marked her wedding half a century before. Elizabeth Stuart had been born when Queen Elizabeth i was on the throne of England and Shakespeare was writing; she had lived through the Thirty Years' War in Europe and the English Civil War; she had learned of the execution of her brother King Charles i and had seen the Restoration of her nephew King Charles ii. Once the most celebrated beauty in England, she had lived abroad ever since her marriage, and after fifty years the popular legend of the Protestant heroine, exiled, widowed and afflicted, had begun to fade. Charles ii did not attend her state funeral in Westminster Abbey, and her passing was generally noted with more curiosity than regret. 'It is a pity she lived not a few hours more, to die upon her wedding day,' observed her London host, Lord Leicester, 'and that there is not as good a poet to make her epitaph as Dr Donne, who wrote her Epithalamium upon that day, unto St Valentine.'

Thirteen children had been born of Elizabeth Stuart's St Valentine's Day marriage; of the six who outlived her, only Prince Rupert was in England to take part in the torchlit funeral procession which made its way up the river Thames by barge on the night of 17 February. Yet in Westminster Abbey, close by the royal vault in which the 'most high, most mighty and excellent Princess Elizabeth, late Queen of Bohemia' was interred with her ancestors, her youngest daughter's son would one day be crowned King George I, and after him, throughout the coming generations, her direct descendants would be Kings and Queens of England. In his 'Epithalamium, or Marriage Song', written in 1612, John Donne had likened Elizabeth Stuart to a phoenix; it was to prove a prophetic image.

The beautiful and remarkable woman from whom Great Britain's royal line was to spring was born in Scotland on 19 August 1596, and named Elizabeth in honour of her godmother, Queen Elizabeth I of England. Her parents, young King James VI and Queen Anne of Scotland, ever anxious for the good graces of the ageing, childless Queen of England, expressed their hope 'that this Princess may have the name of her Majesty and be patronized with her favour', and Elizabeth I, after a token demurral, consented.

The Queen of England was nearing her sixtieth birthday when she received word of the birth of a daughter to the King of Scotland. In 1566, as a young woman of thirty, she had learned of King James's own birth; according to one report the news had upset her greatly, and she had burst out, 'The Queen of Scots is lighter of a fair son, and I am of barren stock.' She had, however, recovered her equanimity in time to stand godmother to the baby prince and send a golden font as a christening gift. Now James was himself a father twice over, while she remained a virgin, with neither son nor daughter to inherit her kingdom. Cosmetics and compliments could not prevent the advance of time; the day was approaching when Elizabeth I would no longer rule England. Yet still she resolutely refused to name her heir. To do so, she said, would be to hold her winding-sheet up before her eyes; she herself, in her sister's reign, had known what it was to be the heir to the throne of England, the object of plotters' and flatterers' schemes. 'And so shall never be my successor,' she declared to Parliament. Who that successor was to be remained a subject for speculation, and on the part of her young cousin King James VI of Scotland, for hope. At every opportunity he reaffirmed his dutiful devotion to his ageing royal relation; even her execution of his mother, Mary, Queen of Scots, in 1587, brought no real protest from James. His first-born child, Prince Henry, was made Queen Elizabeth's godson; now, on the birth of his daughter, the Queen of England was once more humbly applied to, 'to accept their dedication of this child to her, to give name to her, and to dispose of all things therein as she shall like.'

At the christening of the Princess Elizabeth, which took place in 'winter season and ill weather', on 28 November 1596, the English ambassador, Robert Bowes, stood proxy for his queen. 'The whole honours in the solemnization of all the ceremonies were given alone to her Majesty,' he assured her in his report of the occasion. It was he who on behalf of the royal godmother carried the baby to the font and spoke her name, after which Lyon Herald proclaimed her to all as the Lady Elizabeth, first daughter of Scotland.

The birth of King James's son and heir, Prince Henry, two years earlier, had been greeted by the Scots as 'a great comfort and matter of joy to the whole people', but the arrival of this baby princess was considered of less importance to the future of the House of Stuart. Few guests were invited to the baptism in the chapel of Holyrood-house, and the Queen of England failed to send a gift to her little namesake, somewhat to Robert Bowes's embarrassment. King James had ordered new socks of crimson velvet laced with gold for himself and liveries of scarlet cloth for members of his household, and fiddlers and drummers were appointed to make music, but in comparison with the elaborate christening of Prince Henry in September 1594, the King of Scotland's daughter was baptized with little ceremony.

Among those summoned to her christening banquet were the chief dignitaries of Edinburgh; their gift to the princess, made on behalf of the whole town, was a promise of ten thousand Scots marks, to be paid at the time of her marriage, written in golden letters and presented in a golden casket. It was a significant gesture. This second child had been born not to rule but to marry; as a baby of four months old she had received her first wedding gift.

The match which her father had made with the Princess Anne of Denmark was proving more successful, in both dynastic and personal terms, than might have been expected. James VI was himself the child of a notoriously unhappy marriage; the rift between his mother, Mary, Queen of Scots, and his corrupt and dissolute father, Lord Darnley, had culminated in Darnley's murder, in which Mary was thought by many to have been an accomplice. After the age of thirteen months James never saw either of his parents again. He grew up timid and ungainly, with an undisguised attraction for beautiful young men, yet his relationship with his frivolous blonde Danish bride was, at the time of Elizabeth's birth, more than formal, as successive additions to the royal nursery were to prove.

In accordance with tradition, Queen Anne was not permitted to look after her own children. 'The custody and bringing-up of the King's daughter is committed to Lord Livingstone,' the Queen of England was informed a fortnight after Princess Elizabeth's christening. 'The Princess is sent to Linlithgow to remain there for such time as shall be found convenient.' Linlithgow, birthplace of Mary, Queen of Scots, was the most beautiful of the Scottish royal palaces. Situated between the capital, Edinburgh, and Stirling, where Elizabeth's brother Prince Henry was being brought up by the Earl of Mar, traditional guardian of the heir to the throne, it was a many-turreted castle of elegant proportions, 'a palace of pleasance', such as the French nobility had emulated in their châteaux on the Loire. On his marriage King James had given the lordship of Linlithgow to his queen; now, for the seven years of her Scottish childhood, it was to be the residence of his daughter.

The Keeper of Linlithgow, Lord Livingstone, had been most anxious to obtain the custody of the Princess Elizabeth, 'that thereby he may the better match the Earl of Mar, now in quarrel with him,' Robert Bowes reported dryly to Elizabeth 1. There was considerable doubt about Livingstone's suitability for the office, since his wife, the former Lady Eleanor Hay, was known to be 'an obstinate Papist', but King James publicly showed his satisfaction with Livingstone's performance of his duties by creating him Earl of Linlithgow at the baptism of Prince Charles in 1600. That Elizabeth herself was happy in his care was demonstrated by her lifelong affection for members of his family and household; the favour which she showed in later life towards the second Earl of Linlithgow was explained by the fact that she had had her 'first breeding in his father's house'.

The infancy of the Princess Elizabeth was very different from her father's troubled childhood. She passed her early years in an atmosphere of security; her emotional, as well as material, needs were attended to. 'Babies [dolls] to play her with' featured regularly in the treasurer's account-books, and at the age of six she received as a New Year's gift from her parents a charming present for a little girl – a velvet case containing combs. The fair hair for which she was later to be celebrated was evidently well cared for; another entry in the account-books recorded the expenditure of eight Scots shillings on a 'birse', or brush, 'to stroke her hair'. Considerable sums were spent on her clothes. Rich dresses of crimson and yellow satin, Spanish frieze and taffeta and figured velvet were provided; her woollen caps were trimmed with lace and there was coloured ribbon on the sleeves of her night-gown. Bright-coloured crepes were purchased, and gold and silver fringing, to be put about her neck.

In 1598 she was joined at Linlithgow by a baby sister, the Lady Margaret, but this second princess lived only two years. Then, in 1600, Queen Anne gave birth to a second son, Prince Charles. He seemed too delicate to live, and was accordingly baptized without delay. None of the three children who were to follow lived beyond their second year, but 'Baby Charles' struggled, backward and ailing, through his infancy, and survived. Throughout his childhood Prince Charles was to present a feeble contrast to his lively, charming elder brother and sister, and to James 1 he remained 'Baby Charles' all his life.

In Prince Henry, King James had an heir of great promise. 'In the surety of my son consisteth my surety,' he wrote to the boy's guardian when Henry was a year old, but Lord Mar needed no reminding of the heavy responsibilities of his hereditary office. His mother the dowager countess, 'an ancient, virtuous and severe lady', had the care of the prince from the cradle; formidable though she was, as he grew from babyhood Henry 'did not only reverence her, but also love her most dearly'. Under the devoted auspices of the Mar family

Henry showed early signs of a noble and heroic spirit. When asked as a small child which was his favourite musical instrument he answered promptly 'A trumpet.' From the age of seven he was encouraged to take a princely interest in physical activities and sports, learning to ride, sing, dance, leap, shoot and toss his pike, and, most important of all, being instructed in the use of arms. At six years old his New Year's gifts from King James and Queen Anne included a set of golf-clubs.

By the time 'Baby Charles' was born, only three more years of life in Scotland remained to Prince Henry and Princess Elizabeth. The winter season of their father's fortunes was about to give way to a triumphant spring. 'St George surely rides upon a towardly riding horse, where I am daily bursting in daunting a wild unruly colt,' James vi once complained: he believed his Scottish subjects to be 'a far more barbarous and stiff-necked people' than the orderly English whom he longed to rule. Year by year the ageing Elizabeth i steadfastly refused to name her heir, yet in her dealings with her cousin of Scotland she gave James good grounds for hope. More encouraging even than Elizabeth's half-hints and oblique allusions was the correspondence in cypher which Robert Cecil, her chief minister, carried on with James from the spring of 1601. Cecil's letters were kept strictly secret from Elizabeth, for, as he later discreetly put it, the queen's advancing age, 'joined to the jealousy of her sex, might have moved her to think ill of that which helped to preserve her'. The way was being made clear for a transfer of power as soon as the queen was dead. To the timid, cautious, homosexual King James vi was to fall the prize which generations of virile Stuart kings had coveted – the throne of England.

'This morning, at about 3 o'clock,' wrote an English diarist on 24 May 1603, 'her Majesty departed this life mildly like a lamb, easily like a ripe apple from the tree . . . and I doubt not but that she is amongst the royal Saints in heaven in eternal joys'. James Stuart was proclaimed King James i of England at Whitehall Gate at ten o'clock that same morning. 'The proclamation was heard with great expectation and silent joy, no great shouting,' the diarist

6

recorded. Elizabeth Stuart was now a Princess of England, and her secluded life at Linlithgow was at an end.

To the nine-year-old Prince Henry, the king sent a fond letter, explaining 'That I see you not before my parting, impute it to this great occasion, wherein time is so precious,' and bidding him : 'Let not this news make you proud or insolent, for a King's son and heir was ye before, and no more are ye now.' On 5 April the new King James I of England set off on his triumphant progress south, to be followed, at a more leisurely pace, by his wife and children.

Among the various ladies of honour who hurried to Scotland to present themselves to their new queen and attend her on her way into England were two Englishwomen who were to play a central part in Elizabeth's new life, Lady Harington and her married daughter Lady Bedford. Distressingly, at this great moment in her life Queen Anne gave birth prematurely to a stillborn son. On the night before her departure the Princess Elizabeth was also found to be unwell, but in her case the ailment had no serious effects, and at the beginning of June she set out as planned on the first great journey of her life.

The 'charges and expenses of the Lady Elizabeth's grace' on this occasion amounted to £196 5s, quite apart from the cost of her grooms, carriages and horses. She travelled by easy stages, joining the faster-moving Queen Anne at appointed stopping-places along the route. Berwick-on-Tweed was the scene of an important meeting; there the Countess of Kildare, appointed by Queen Anne as the princess's English governess, was presented to her for the first time. 'My Lady Kildare comes after with the young Princess,' ran a contemporary report of Queen Anne's progress, 'and as I think will not be at York before Monday, being the 13th of June.' At the medieval city of York, Elizabeth was presented with a purse full of gold angels, whilst at Leicester, which she reached before the queen and Prince Henry, who had made a detour to visit Ashby, she was received by the mayor, and given a quantity of wines and a large sugar-loaf, costing thirty-three shillings and ninepence.

Three weeks later, on Saturday, 25 June, Elizabeth had her first sight of the house which was to be her home for much of her childhood. Combe Abbey, near Coventry in Warwickshire, was the ancient and beautiful residence of the Haringtons, a cloistered English country house very different in architecture and atmosphere from the Scottish castle where she had spent her infancy. Combe Abbey, more than any other building, was to be associated with Elizabeth Stuart; after her death her portraits and those of her children would hang there undisturbed for centuries.

On this occasion, however, the Princess Elizabeth paid only a brief visit to her future home; her presence was required at Windsor, which she reached on 30 June, in advance of the king and queen and Prince Henry. She arrived there in great style, accompanied by her governess, the Lady Kildare, in the same litter, and attended by thirty horsemen. It was noted that the little princess 'had her trumpets and formalities as well as the rest'. The flourish of trumpets which greeted Elizabeth at Windsor could be said to have heralded the beginning of her new life. No longer was she merely the Lady Elizabeth, first daughter of Scotland; the pretty fair-haired child who had been so christened, in 'winter season and ill weather', six years before, was henceforth to be brought up as a Princess of England.

CHAPTER TWO
Promised Land

The new King of England saw himself 'like a poor man wandering about forty years in a wilderness and barren soil and now arrived at the land of promise'. James I believed his new realm to be a land of plenty, and he proposed to enjoy its fruits. Before he had even arrived in London he had bestowed an extravagant number of knighthoods on his followers; his refusal to court the common people who came flocking to see him was only equalled by his imprudent generosity towards the individuals whom he favoured. At the time of James's accession the English crown was rich in the people's love but poor in financial resources; as his extravagant reign progressed it was to become increasingly impoverished in both.

In the early summer of 1603, however, the king and his family were enthusiastically welcomed by their new subjects. The diarist who recorded the death of Queen Elizabeth and the proclamation of King James had expressed the feelings of many when he wrote, 'I think the sorrow for her Majesty's departure was so deep in many hearts they could not suddenly show any great joy, though it could not be any less than exceeding great for the succession of so worthy a King.' After so many decades of uncertainty over the succession, the presence of a king with a well-stocked nursery was a source of relief to all loyal Englishmen.

The nine-year-old heir to the throne, Prince Henry, quickly made a good impression upon his father's new subjects. Soon after his arrival, on 2 July, he was installed as a Knight of the Garter at Windsor, and was much commended 'for divers his quick witty answers, princely carriage and reverend performing his obeisance at the Altar, all which seemed very strange unto them and the rest of the beholders, considering his tender age'. The glittering celebrations gave a foretaste of splendours to come at the Jacobean court; one awed young onlooker reported that there was 'such an infinite company of lords and ladies and so great a Court as I think I shall never see the like again'. Princess Elizabeth was allowed to enter the great hall and see the knights of St George, of whom her elder brother was now one, seated at their dinner.

Among those present at Windsor was the French ambassador, M. de Beaumont; King James took the opportunity to remind him that a double marriage was talked of, between Prince Henry and a daughter of King Henry IV and the Princess Elizabeth and the dauphin. Gesturing to his daughter, James informed the Frenchman that Elizabeth had been shown the dauphin's portrait and had fallen in love with it. De Beaumont was subsequently given the chance to form his own impressions of the child who might one day become Queen of France. The meeting took place in her mother's drawing-room; Elizabeth had clearly been well schooled beforehand, for the ambassador found her 'very well-bred' and 'rather serious than gay', and thought she had a gentle disposition. In looks, he thought her tall for her age, and 'handsome enough'.

After the varied excitements of her sojourn at Windsor Elizabeth remained with the court for several weeks; it was at this time that she paid her first visit to the Tudor river-palace of Hampton Court. Thereafter she travelled on to another of Henry VIII's former residences, Oatlands, in Surrey, where a nursery establishment was formed for Prince Henry and herself. The ten-year-old Garter Knight was provided with 'so many to attend upon him in every office, as was thought fitting for his years'; he and Elizabeth had at first seventy servants to wait on them. During this brief but happy period for Elizabeth, the Venetian secretary paid a visit to the two children. He reported that Prince Henry was ceremonious beyond his years and, though quick-witted, conducted himself with great gravity. The Venetia continued: 'Through an interpreter he gave me a long discourse on his exercises, dancing, tennis, the chase. He then himself conducted me down one flight of stairs and up another to visit the Princess. . . . They both said they meant to learn Italian.'

The prince and princess did not remain together at Oatlands for long. The discovery of the first of several plots against King James, in the autumn of 1603, led to the removal of Lady Kildare from her post as Elizabeth's governess, when her second husband was found to have been implicated in the conspiracy. On 19 October 1603, a Privy Seal order was issued, stating that the king had decided 'to commit the keeping and educating of the Lady Elizabeth our daughter to the Lord Harington and the lady his wife'. £1,500 was to be the basic yearly allowance for her keep. Elizabeth, now seven years old, was sent to Exton Hall in Rutland and from there to the Haringtons' residence of Combe Abbey. In this splendid mansion she was to spend most of her remaining childhood years.

Combe Abbey had been founded as a Cistercian monastery in the twelfth century, and it retained such monastic features as cloisters and a belfry. There was a park and a lake in the grounds, while inside the house the Haringtons had modernized the fine rooms and galleries to provide Jacobean standards of beauty and comfort for the royal resident. Acting as host and guardian to the king's only daughter was to prove an expensive honour for Lord Harington. A considerable household was provided to look after the princess; her Scottish nurse, Alison Hay, who had attended her since her babyhood, was still at her side, as were a personal physician, tutors, a dancing-master and a music-master, in addition to her French maid, two liveried footmen, three bedchamber women, a sempstress, a laundress, grooms of the presence chamber and the bedchamber, and, very important to a child who had inherited her father's love of hunting, grooms to care for the nineteen or twenty horses in her stable.

Little is known of the details of Elizabeth's daily life during her childhood at Combe Abbey. A much-quoted source of pretty anec-dotes purporting to have been written by one of her ladies in later years and published in the following century is now generally accepted as spurious. What is certain, however, is that compared with such illustrious women as her godmother Queen Elizabeth I, the Princess Elizabeth received a limited formal education. Though King James was a scholar and a noted author, with interests ranging from poetry to demonology, he was no believer in the higher education of women. Queen Anne was not clever, and her patronage of such artists and writers as Inigo Jones and Ben Jonson stemmed not from a disinterested appreciation of the arts, but from her own pursuit of pleasure. The daughter of this ill-assorted couple was by no means unintelligent, but her mind was never disciplined. At Combe Abbey she learned all that was necessary for a Christian princess, which consisted chiefly of excellent French and good Italian, music, dancing, and a great deal of religious knowledge. For a time the composer Dr John Bull, to whom the National Anthem is attributed, had the charge of her musical education, and she showed a talent for playing the virginals, but riding and hunting were to remain Elizabeth's favourite occupations from her childhood into her old age.

Her handwriting, which was to degenerate into a swift-moving scrawl in her adult life, so that her letters were often 'fearfully scribbled and blotted', was in her early childhood a carefully formed script of stiff, upright letters between ruled red lines. She expressed herself with formal courtesy, but the style could not hide the strength of her love for her elder brother Henry. Her earliest existing letter, probably written soon after her departure from Oatlands in 1603, was addressed to him. It ran, 'My dear and worthy brother, I most kindly salute you, desiring to hear of your health, from whom though I am now removed far away, none shall ever be nearer in affection than Your most loving sister Elizabeth.' A later effort, written in French, began somewhat plaintively, 'My letters follow you everywhere. I hope they may be as acceptable to you as they are frequent.' Her constant theme was her regret at being parted from him and her eagerness for their next meeting.

Henry's replies, to his 'Beloved Madam Elizabeth', echoed her desire that they might be together, but as became his superior age, sex and status, he was more philosophical than she about it. 'You know that those who love each other best cannot be always glued together,' he reminded her on one occasion. However, a contemporary description of the prince's character affirmed that 'as for the Lady Elizabeth his sister, he loved her always so dearly that he desired to see her always by him'. They visited each other and rode together as often as they were allowed, 'otherwise he did send often to enquire of her health, with divers infallible signs and tokens of his great love and affection'.

The waning of King James I's initial popularity did not lessen his subjects' affection for his children. On the contrary, as the monarch's reputation declined, the love of loyal Englishmen for Prince Henry and Princess Elizabeth seemed to increase. It was to Elizabeth that the conspirators in the great 'Powder Plot' would have turned for their next ruler, had they succeeded in their plans to blow up the Parliament House and rid the kingdom of James Stuart.

Many English Catholics had expected that the coming of King James would bring an easing of restrictions on their religion. Queen Anne's personal sympathies had appeared to receive public confirmation when she refused to take the sacrament after the Anglican fashion at the coronation service, and James himself was known to favour tolerance towards his Catholic subjects. His initial leniency in lifting recusancy fines was, however, short-lived; under the influence of Robert Cecil, whose constant fear was the spread of foreign agents, the king gave his consent to a tightening of anti-Catholic laws. And these, as one Jesuit put it, proved to be 'the spurs that set those gentlemen upon that furious and fiery course which they afterwards fell into'.

'Those gentlemen' included Robert Catesby, his cousin Thomas Winter, Thomas Percy and an explosives expert named Guy, or Guido, Fawkes. Whilst the nine-year-old Princess Elizabeth was busy with her books at Combe Abbey, writing little notes to her elder brother, or riding in the Warwickshire woods, the conspirators were devising a plot which, had it succeeded, would have left her fatherless and changed the course of her life.

Gunpowder was secreted in barrels in a cellar beneath the Parliament House. When the nobility and members of the Lower House were assembled for the opening of Parliament on 5 November 1605, and the king and prince had entered, a mighty explosion was to take place which would have 'blown up all at a clap', in Cecil's picturesque phrase. With the king and Prince Henry thus disposed of, the plotters intended to seize 'the Lady Elizabeth, the King's daughter, in Warwickshire, and presently proclaim her Queen'. Initially they intended to hold her at the house of Robert Catesby's mother, at Ashby St Legers. As Guy Fawkes subsequently confessed under torture, Elizabeth would have been forced to change her religion and be brought up a Catholic, though he could not say 'who should have had the government and education of her' until the time came for her to be married off to a suitable Catholic husband. Clearly the plotters had only a vague conception of what the Lady Elizabeth's future role was to be, but they had little doubt that she would be willingly accepted as Queen Elizabeth II by the English people.

Lord Harington acted promptly when it became apparent that danger threatened the king and his family. Fearing that rebellion was in the air, Harington sent his royal charge away to Coventry, where a safe lodging awaited her in the house of a Mr Hopkins, a well-to-do resident of Earl Street. The rebels, it was reported, arrived at Combe Abbey 'but two hours too late to have seized upon the person of the Lady Elizabeth's grace'. The princess remained securely out of the way while Harington, having first informed Robert Cecil of his intended course of action, rode out with Sir Fulke Greville to take up arms against the conspirators.

With their plans betrayed and Guy Fawkes taken red-handed amongst the powder kegs, the plotters fled to Holbeach, on the Staffordshire borders. There they were swiftly surrounded, and on 8 November, in the final flurry of shooting, Catesby and Percy, fighting back to back, were killed by the same musket-shot. It was a fittingly dramatic climax to the plot which might have altered the course of English history.

Elizabeth's own comment on the affair was recorded by her

guardian. 'What a Queen should I have been by this means!' she exclaimed. 'I had rather have been with my royal father in the Parliament House, than wear his crown on such condition.' Her heroic reaction did not prevent the frightening disturbance of her daily life from taking its toll; three months afterwards, shortly before the gruesome execution of Guy Fawkes, Lord Harington recorded that the residents of his household at Combe Abbey were still unwell and in low spirits. The princess herself, he wrote, 'hath not yet recovered the surprise, and is very ill and troubled'. For the nine-year-old Elizabeth Stuart the Gunpowder Plot had provided an early lesson in the vulnerability of royalty.

Prince Henry had had an even more fortunate escape than his sister. The princess wrote him a note in her very best handwriting, congratulating him on his happy deliverance from danger. 'If the Lord be for us, who can be against us?' she declared piously. 'In his keeping I will not fear what any man can do.' Another of Henry's correspondents on this occasion was a young German prince of the same age as Elizabeth – the dark-complexioned Frederick, elder son of the Elector Palatine. Like Elizabeth, Frederick addressed Prince Henry in French, expressing horror at the wicked plot so happily averted. Like Elizabeth, Frederick was growing up fast; that he might one day call Prince Henry 'brother-in-law' was a possibility which must already have occurred to interested parties in the Protestant Palatinate.

The great conspiracy had given the heavily burdened Lord Harington yet further proof of the weight of his responsibilities as Elizabeth's guardian. His witty cousin Sir John Harington observed, 'Lord Harington of Exton doth much fatigue himself with the royal charge of the Princess Elizabeth, and midst all the foolery of these times, hath much labour to preserve his own wisdom and sobriety.' His burden of care cannot have been made lighter by Elizabeth's expedition to her parents' court in the summer of 1606. The occasion was the visit of her uncle, King Christian iv of Denmark, brother of the queen. For Queen Anne herself it was a difficult time, since just before his arrival she gave birth to a daughter, Sophia, who lived only a few hours; but for Elizabeth the taste of court life was delightful. While James I and Prince Henry met the visiting king at Gravesend, Elizabeth and her little brother Charles awaited their arrival on the landing-place at Greenwich Palace, and subsequently accompanied the two monarchs when they went to visit her mother in her chamber. 'Wild riot, excess and devastation of time and temperament' were the modern evils against which Lord Harington's cousin inveighed, and the words gave an apt description of the court of the unbridled King James and his frivolous queen. From James's slobbering jokes and lecherous petting of his handsome favourites to Queen Anne's endless round of feasts and masques, 'balling and night waking', there was much at the Jacobean court that might corrupt a child. Yet the response of both Elizabeth and Henry, and later of Charles, to their parents' example proved to be one of reaction and not imitation; much as Elizabeth loved pleasure, her upbringing by the godly Haringtons had taught her from an early age to value virtue and maintain her dignity. Prince Henry, for all his love of sports and games, was celebrated for his serious-mindedness, and as he grew to maturity he was increasingly to rebel against his father's judgement – as was shown in his famous scathing comment on the imprisonment of Sir Walter Raleigh : 'Who but my father would keep such a bird in a cage?' Elizabeth was to prove Lord Harington's anxiety unfounded; he had taught her well. With ten-year-old innocence she thoroughly enjoyed this rare glimpse of public life, and her letters to her brother referred to it with delight after her return to the quiet of Combe Abbey.

As Elizabeth grew older she was to have more such treats. For the Christmas of 1607, when she was eleven, she was allowed to return to court, and there, to her delight, Prince Henry was also staying. The French ambassador, M. le Fevre de la Boderie, took the opportunity to study the princess, for whom a marriage with the dauphin was still talked of. His report was very favourable. He found her beautiful, graceful, full of virtue and merit and proficient in the French language, which she spoke far better than her elder brother. 'I assure you', the ambassador reported, 'it will not be her fault if she is not Dauphine – and she might have worse fancies – for she is not at all put out when it is mentioned to her.' Elizabeth Stuart's prospects seemed very bright at Christmas 1607. Not only could she look forward to a future in which she might one day become Queen of France; she could do so with the additional pleasure of knowing that her beloved Henry would have a part in that destiny, for her elder brother had promised that he would only agree to a French match for himself if she were married to the dauphin. Thus, though married, they would remain close to each other, sharing a double alliance in which private emotions might be happily combined with political expediency.

Elizabeth did not appear to be spoiled by the attention paid to her as she grew up. 'Why should vain joys us transport?/Earthly pleasures are but short,' she wrote in 1609, in a religious poem which she dedicated to her pious guardian. Another verse of the laboured work ran,

> God is only excellent
> Let up to him our love be sent;
> Whose desires are set or bent
> On aught else shall much repent.

She had evidently not inherited her father's gift for poetry, but the sentiments must have pleased Lord Harington. Elizabeth Stuart's characteristic liveliness, which she was to retain throughout the misfortunes of her adult life, did not ever detract from the strict sense of propriety which the Haringtons had instilled into her.

King James showed considerable satisfaction with his only surviving daughter. He frequently made her presents of jewellery, clothes, riding equipment and other finery suitable to a young princess, and he took pleasure in her visits to court. Early in 1609 Elizabeth was allowed to be present at several memorable royal events : in February she watched one of Ben Jonson's ballets, performed in honour of a young nobleman's marriage, and in April she accompanied her father, mother and brothers to the opening of 'Britain's Burse', a group of shops in the Strand, where they were entertained with 'pleasant speeches, gifts and ingenious devices'. On 23 June she witnessed a less pleasant spectacle – a confrontation between a bear, which had killed a child, and some of the lions from the Tower menagerie. Elizabeth's passion for little animals and birds, and her ownership of a series of dogs, parrots and monkeys, did not hinder her from thoroughly enjoying blood-sports : 'To the keeper of Nonsuch Great Park, for his fee, her grace killing a doe there, 20s' ran one entry in her account book.

In January 1610, when she was thirteen, Elizabeth had the delightful experience of being entertained by her brother Henry, at St James's Palace. First, on Twelfth Night, there was the great tournament, Prince Henry's Barriers, at which the youthful prince distinguished himself, to the great admiration of the beholders, who included his adoring sister. The speeches written for the occasion by Ben Jonson concluded with some lines about the royal children; addressing King James, the figure of Merlin first approached Prince Henry with the words,

> And this young Knight, that now puts forth so soon
> Into the world, shall in your names achieve
> More garlands for this State, and shall relieve
> Your cares in government.

Of the weakly second son, Prince Charles, the Welsh magician said,

> . . . while that young Lord
> Shall second him in arms, and shake a sword
> And lance against the foes of God and you.

Addressed to one who, as king, was destined to bear arms against the rebellious subjects of the English Crown, those were strangely prophetic lines. But when Merlin turned to Elizabeth, his words were yet more appropriate. Calling her 'That most princely maid, whose form might call/The world to war', he uttered the phrase, 'She shall be Mother of Nations.' At the time it passed as a pretty compliment, but it was to prove a prediction worthy of King Arthur's wizard.

More enchantment was to follow : at Prince Henry's banquet the next evening Elizabeth presided with her brother, and, assisted by the king, presented the prizes to the victors of the tournament. After dinner the king retired, but Henry and Elizabeth proceeded to watch a play, and then returned to the supper-table to find a most remarkable feast laid out. Round the 120-foot table Henry solemnly led his sister twice; together they gazed with wonder at the fountains of rosewater, and incredible sweetmeats in the shape of flower-gardens, windmills, mythical creatures and even the constellations. Not until three o'clock in the morning, after a most undignified scramble by the assembled company eager for souvenirs of the gorgeous confectionery, did the gathering break up.

The princess was growing up fast. She had her own royal barge to travel in, and rooms in the part of Whitehall Palace known as the Cockpit were put at her disposal for her use during her increasingly frequent visits to court. She was there again in May 1610, for a most important event – the creation of Henry as Prince of Wales.

As the civic procession escorting Henry into London moved up the river towards Whitehall Stairs on 31 May, so many spectators took to the water in boats that it seemed as though the Thames, even at high tide, could not contain them all, while the river banks on either side were overloaded with hundreds more onlookers. The barges of the aldermen of London and City companies made a colourful sight, 'decked with banners, streamers and ensigns, and sundry sorts of loud-sounding instruments', and beside the Lord Mayor's barge there floated two mechanical sea-creatures, 'one in fashion of a whale, the other like a dolphin', bearing gorgeously dressed deities on their backs. So that the king and the rest of the royal family might have a good view the barges passed along beside Whitehall Palace, where the king and queen stood with Elizabeth and Charles at a window of the privy gallery. As the sixteen-year-old Henry alighted from his barge and bade farewell to the Lord Mayor and aldermen there could be no doubting his popularity with his father's subjects.

Such a great occasion called for the most lavish of masques, and in the evening of 5 June Elizabeth took part for the first time in one of her mother's entertainments. Called *Tethys Festival; or the Queen's*

Wake, it was written by a groom of the Privy Chamber named Samuel Daniel, with Inigo Jones as 'Architictor', and it starred Queen Anne as Tethys, Queen of the Ocean and wife of Neptune, attended with 'thirteen nymphs of several rivers'. Elizabeth appeared as 'the lovely Nymph of Stately Thames'. The various nymphs were wonderfully dressed, with shells and coral in their hair; 'their upper garments had the bodice of sky-coloured taffetas, for lightness, all embroidered with maritime invention'. Little Prince Charles, now ten years old, came on as Zephirus, 'in a short robe of green satin embroidered with golden flowers', with silver wings and a garland of multi-coloured flowers in his hair. The fireworks which concluded the following evening's investiture celebrations could not have been more showy and glittering than Elizabeth's first court masque.

Since Prince Henry was interested in ships and navigation, his adoring sister was too. In September of 1610 she paid a visit to the 'most goodly ship for war' the *Prince Royal*, which had been two years in the building under the auspices of Phineas Pett, at Woolwich. Pett himself described how 'numbers of people continually resorted to Woolwich, of all sorts, both Nobles, Gentry and Citizens, and from all parts of the country', which, he added ruefully, 'was no small charge to me, in giving daily entertainment to all comers'. By 24 September, all was ready for the royal launching. A stand, securely railed off, had been set up for the king, queen and royal children to watch the ceremony from, and, in Pett's words, 'nothing was omitted that could be imagined any ways necessary both for ease and entertainment'. The king and Prince Henry arrived at the shipyard at about eleven o'clock in the morning; James was feeling unwell after a surfeit of grapes, but was determined not to miss the launching. After lunch the queen, with Elizabeth and 'Baby Charles', arrived and with their entourage they took their places. Everything had been planned with the utmost care; drummers and trumpeters were positioned on the poop and foc'sle of the great ship, and the wind instruments by them, 'so that nothing was wanting to so great a royalty that could be desired'. But disappointment followed. The *Prince Royal* started to move – but 'the dock gates pent her in so straight that she stuck fast between them'. There was nothing to be done. The assembled company had to go home again, the king making it very clear to Pett that he was most upset 'to be frustrate of his expectation, coming on purpose, though very ill at ease, to have done me honour', as Pett recounted. Prince Henry, who was to have launched the ship himself, and performed the ceremony of drinking wine from a standing-cup, giving the *Prince Royal* her name, and then flinging the cup overboard, was more helpful. He stayed on for some time after his family had departed, discussing with Pett and the Lord Admiral what was to be done. Finally Henry left, with a promise to return after midnight, which he duly did, in spite of the fact that a great storm had blown up. 'His invincible spirit, daunted with nothing, made little account of it', and he reached the shipyard about an hour before high tide. Thus he was on board the *Prince Royal* as she slipped easily away, 'till she came clear afloat in the middle of the Channel', and standing upon the poop he performed the christening ceremony. And so the *Prince Royal*, which less than two years later was to carry the newly-wed Elizabeth to her new home, was finally launched.

The subject of Elizabeth's marriage continued to arouse speculation and hopes at home and abroad. In the spring of 1610 her young kinsman Frederick Ulrich of Brunswick, son of Queen Anne's sister Elizabeth and the Duke of Brunswick, had arrived in England; officially he was on an educational grand tour, but there was no doubt that the possibility of a match with the King of England's daughter was in his mind, as it was in his mother's. Other eligible princes had also visited King James's court, and been richly entertained; then, in September 1610, Elizabeth's first real proposal arrived. It was made on behalf of the King of Sweden's heir, the military-minded Prince Gustavus Adolphus. Though rich enough, and Protestant, the blond Swedish prince was unacceptable to the English royal family, since his country was at war with Queen Anne's native Denmark. Other suitors were not deterred by Gustavus Adolphus's rebuff however, and within a month Prince Maurice of Orange had offered himself as a husband for Elizabeth Stuart.

In May 1610 Henry IV of France was murdered. Not only was it a great shock to Prince Henry, who had developed a considerable regard for the French king; it also meant an end of the plans for a double marriage between a son and daughter of Henry IV and the English princess and prince. The widowed French queen, Marie de Médicis, preferred to look to mighty Catholic Spain for her elder children's spouses. And so the way was left clear for the series of hopeful candidates who presented themselves as suitors to the King of England's beautiful daughter.

Within the realm there was no man of high enough birth to match with the Stuart princess. Two Howard contenders for her hand, the Earl of Northampton and Lord Howard de Walden, were regarded as out of the question. 'The overture of a marriage for the blessed Lady Elizabeth with the Prince of Savoy' was to be no more fortunate in its eventual outcome, though this offer merited serious consideration. The Duke of Savoy proposed that his son Victor Amadeus should become the husband of Elizabeth, while – and here there was a notable advantage for the devoted brother and sister – Prince Henry should marry his daughter the Princess of Savoy. A good deal was said and written on the subject of this offer, but few reflected upon its relative merits as cogently as the captive Sir Walter Raleigh.

The great Elizabethan courtier, poet and sea-dog had at the beginning of King James's reign incurred the royal disfavour, and ever since 1603 Raleigh had been a prisoner in the Tower. After an initial fit of despair, during which he attempted suicide, he had made a magnificent effort to come to terms with his new condition. Tried and sentenced to death for treason, his execution was continually suspended, and though officially a dead man in the eyes of the law, he gave every proof of remaining exuberantly alive. His second son was born in the Tower, and he exercised his mental faculties with equal success. He conducted scientific experiments in a converted henhouse in the lieutenant's garden; he was visited by leading scholars of the day, so that his rooms in the Bloody Tower took on something of the atmosphere of a university, and he wrote prolifically. The mature and intelligent Prince Henry was one of his most valuable supporters; it was he who encouraged Raleigh to begin his *History of the World*, which the author eventually dedicated to his young royal patron. Henry may have talked of his sister to the prisoner; at all events, Raleigh concerned himself with the question of Elizabeth's marriage, and produced many pages of prose in discussion of it.

'But let us now', wrote Raleigh, 'enter into due consideration of the person of this excellent young princess, the only daughter of our sovereign, the dear beloved sister of our prince, and one of the precious jewels of this kingdom.' He went on to consider 'what increase of honour or dignity, or what great comfort and contentment she can expect or hope for by the benefit of this match'. As the only daughter of one of the mightiest kings of Christendom Elizabeth was, in Raleigh's opinion, 'of higher place and state than the wife of the Duke of Savoy' and 'descended of such royal races as Savoy cannot add any greater grace or glory unto'. Moreover, in person Elizabeth was 'by nature endowed with such princely perfections, both of body and mind, as may well deserve to be reputed a worthy spouse for the greatest monarch of Christendom'. The advantages, Raleigh insisted, would all be on the side of the 'poor Popish Duke of Savoy'. Elizabeth would achieve little in the way of comfort and contentment, uprooted as she would be from her native country, far from her parents, and sent to live in a land 'as far estranged from our nation as any part of Christendom, and as far differing from us in religion as in climate'.

The question of religion was of paramount importance. Under no circumstances would Elizabeth forsake the faith in which she had been brought up; on that point King James was adamant. In choosing a husband for his daughter he had always to bear in mind the English succession. Though he had two sons to succeed him, it was remembered that the crown of Henry VIII had passed to all three of his children in turn, and it was just possible that some day the English would have to look to the offspring of the Princess Elizabeth for their next ruler. Should that day ever come, it would be of the

B

utmost importance that her children had been brought up to be Protestant in their faith and English in their sympathies.

That King James himself did not feel entirely secure about the succession was demonstrated by his dealings with the unfortunate Arbella Stuart. The grand-daughter of the formidable Bess of Hardwick and her second husband, brother of Mary Queen of Scots' consort Lord Darnley, Arbella was not only the first cousin of King James but a great-great-grand-daughter of Henry VII, with a dangerous degree of both Tudor and Stuart blood in her veins. In the previous reign Elizabeth I had sometimes liked to provoke James by reminding him of Arbella's substantial claim to the throne, and after he became king the Lady Arbella continued to cause him unease. He behaved very graciously towards her, and she was on friendly terms with Queen Anne and the Princess Elizabeth, but the cordial relations persisted only as long as Arbella remained unmarried. In 1610, however, as a spinster in her mid-thirties, she fell desperately in love with a much younger man – William Seymour, grandson of Lady Jane Grey's sister Katherine. She could scarcely have made a more unwelcome choice from the king's point of view, since, under the terms of Henry VIII's will, in which the Stuart line had been entirely passed over in favour of the Grey sisters, William Seymour had himself a claim to the throne, as another of Henry VII's descendants. Their marriage was forbidden, but in the summer of 1610 they disobeyed the royal command and were secretly wed. For a time both were placed in confinement – Seymour in the Tower and his bride in a house in Lambeth. In 1611 both managed to escape, but only Seymour got away to the Continent. Arbella was recaptured and sent to the Tower, where she was to remain until her death in 1615. Although she became increasingly frail in both mind and body, she could not be released on account of James's perpetual fear of plots, and she remained safely imprisoned, yet a thorn in his side, throughout the Princess Elizabeth's marriage negotiations.

By the time Arbella Stuart was put in the Tower the girlhood of Elizabeth was coming to an end. Early in 1611, when she was fourteen, an important document was sent to James I from the Duke de

Bouillon; it contained a detailed description of yet another suitor to the English princess. The young man in question was the duke's nephew and ward, Frederick v, the Elector Palatine. Frederick, who was four days older than Elizabeth, appeared to be in every way an admirable character. His morals were impeccable, his appearance agreeable. Dark in colouring, he was physically fit and active, and he was an excellent horseman. It was altogether a most attractive picture that the Duke de Bouillon painted.

The Palatinate, which consisted of two separate territories in the seventeenth century, was not a large domain, but its ruler enjoyed considerable influence in Europe, as the chief of the seven electors whose privilege it was to elect a new emperor whenever the imperial throne fell vacant. One of Frederick's ancestors, the Elector Rupert III, had himself become emperor in 1401. As a descendant of the houses of Simmern and Wittelsbach, young Frederick was at least the equal of the Stuarts in blood.

It could not be said, however, that the Elector Palatine was a brilliant match for the King of England's only daughter; in the autumn of 1611 the Duke de Bouillon admitted to the English ambassador in Paris that there was some doubt 'whether the Princess would not expect a more chargeable entertainment, in respect of the eminence of her birth, than would stand with the constitution of their state to bear'. Yet despite the young elector's possible shortcomings in actual wealth and rank, he was of undeniably high lineage, and he was, above all, a staunch Protestant. Sir Walter Raleigh, in discussing the question of Elizabeth's marriage, had argued in favour of the young Elector Palatine. Whereas, he pointed out, any children born to Elizabeth and the Prince of Savoy would be 'bred and brought up contrary to her conscience', the elector was 'of our religion', and 'as well born as the Duke of Savoy' to boot.

As Raleigh had loyally maintained, the beautiful and virtuous daughter of the King of England would make 'a worthy spouse for the greatest monarch in Christendom'; at the eleventh hour, when the elector's success seemed assured, that very monarch, the newly-widowed Philip III of Spain, became flatteringly interested in marrying Elizabeth Stuart. The Catholic Queen Anne did all she could to encourage his suit, and as late as July 1612 a special Spanish envoy, Don Pedro de Zuniga, was sent to England to investigate the matrimonial possibilities and was graciously received. Prince Henry, however, spoke out roundly against the match, declaring that 'whosoever should counsel his father to marry his sister to a Catholic prince were a traitor', and though King James was evidently intrigued by the idea of having the mighty King of Spain as his son-in-law, it became apparent to all that such a marriage was out of the question on grounds of religion alone.

When the Spanish envoy Zuniga arrived on his delicate mission, the elector's wooing was already well advanced. In June 1611 his mother, the widowed Electress Louisa Juliana, had written anxiously, 'I fear that our delays will cause us to lose this beautiful princess, and that ... Savoy will carry her off', but she need not have worried. James I, for all his interest in Elizabeth's Catholic suitors, was increasingly convinced that an alliance with the Protestant Frederick would be to the best advantage of his daughter and his kingdom. In Paris the English ambassador Sir Thomas Edmondes returned encouraging answers to the Duke de Bouillon's enquiries about the expectations of the young princess for her 'entertainment' in the Palatinate, and the negotiations proceeded smoothly. King James, Prince Henry and even Queen Anne's brother, King Christian of Denmark, favoured the Elector Palatine, and it was clear that he would be a popular choice with the English people. When the Duke de Bouillon seemed hesitant, fearing the slight of a refusal, King James made it known that other candidates were willing to take that risk, and that Elizabeth could not be kept disengaged indefinitely. The last stage of the negotiations was reached on 16 May 1612, three months before Elizabeth's sixteenth birthday. On that date, in the presence of the Duke de Bouillon, the marriage articles were drawn up in London, and the beautiful and charming daughter of King James of England became contracted to the Elector Palatine, Frederick v.

Elizabeth herself was kept informed of the proceedings. Since the elector had first made known his interest in her, King James informed the duke, she had been guarded from 'hearing the style of love' in any quarter, but now that the wooing had reached its happy conclusion she was allowed to know what was going on. Her marriage portion was to be £40,000, payable within two years of her wedding; the elector was to provide her with a dowry of £10,000 a year if she should survive him and a yearly allowance of £1,500 for her personal expenses. He would be responsible for her household finances, and would pay for the board and wages of forty-nine servants to be appointed by her and brought from England. King James was to pay for her journey to her new home as far as the town of Bacharach and thereafter the elector would be responsible for her travel arrangements. As the princess would be bringing only the modest marriage portion usually given with an Electress Palatine, her father agreed that he would also grant her an annual pension, which would enable her to live in the style that befitted a Princess of England.

It was agreed that the princess should have her own chaplain and continue to worship after the Anglican rite. In the event of children being born to her, the consent of King James was to be obtained before any of them could marry – the safeguarding of the English succession had always to be borne in mind. Elizabeth herself intervened over one aspect of her marriage treaty. It was proposed that part of her revenues should be paid in kind, and not in money, according to the German custom; when her representatives objected to this, Elizabeth overruled them, saying that she preferred to follow the practice of her new country. It was a wise and diplomatic decision for a girl of fifteen to make.

Once the marriage treaty was drawn up and signed, the personal side of Elizabeth Stuart's wooing made speedy progress. In July 1612 the elector sent his steward, Colonel Meinhard von Schönberg, usually known as 'Monsieur Schomberg', over to England; according to one report the German 'was much graced here, and kindly used by the King', but another account declared that he made an unfortunate mix-up in delivering his master's letters, and accidentally presented the Prince of Wales with a tender love-letter while handing the princess the formal note intended for her brother, with the result that he went away 'much discontented'. Rumour had it that Queen Anne was determined to show her displeasure at her daughter's Protestant marriage; it was said that she twitted Elizabeth on her lowly married status, and told her she would be known as 'Goody Palsgrave', 'Palsgrave' being the seventeenth-century English term for a Count or Countess Palatine.

That a higher title might one day be hers had, however, already been anticipated. The Spanish ambassador, Alonso de Velasco, was interested to learn that King James denied the suggestion that Frederick was an inferior alliance for his daughter, saying 'that he doubted not but that his son-in-law would have the title of a King within a few years'. When the ambassador enquired further, he learned that the statement was made 'in respect of the crown of Bohemia, because they pretend it to be elective'. It was alleged that 'France secretly furthereth and helpeth that negotiation,' and the evidence was offered that 'the very private and often conference of the French ambassador with those that have the government of the Count Palatine may justly give cause for suspicion'.

For the time being, however, Frederick was no more – and no less – than the Elector Palatine, Calvinist head of the Union of German Protestant Princes, a somewhat sad-looking fifteen-year-old boy. When Schomberg had delivered his reports of the beautiful princess and the magnificent English court it was hastily decided that young Frederick should refresh his knowledge of dancing and deportment. His tutor accordingly wrote away to the Duke of Württemberg, and requested the loan of his dancing-master for a month, to give Frederick lessons. Further politely worded and neatly written letters were exchanged between the betrothed couple; a train consisting of some 150 people, headed by the Palatine's uncle Prince Henry of Nassau and the ubiquitous Colonel Schomberg, was assembled; and on 17 September all was ready for Frederick's voyage to England.

The young bridegroom expressed a wish that the winds should

prove favourable, but in that he was to be disappointed. Bad weather and storms accompanied his journey from Amsterdam; when, after delays and setbacks, he finally landed at Gravesend at eleven o'clock at night on 16 October, it must have been a relief to all. What followed marked the beginning of the happiest period in Elizabeth Stuart's life.

CHAPTER THREE

The Marriage of Thames
and Rhine

Once the hazardous voyage was over, everything augured well for the
wedding of the Elector Palatine and the Princess Elizabeth. Frederick
began his stay in England in excellent spirits; on being greeted by
the Duke of Lennox on Sunday 18 October, he was reported 'merrily
to have told the Duke that, but to show his obedience, he would
excuse that day's appearance before his Mistress, since he was still
in his travelling-dress. However, he was bidden to see the king, and
so, despite his clothes, he and his party set out for Whitehall by
water.

As they came up the Thames to the Tower eighty guns were shot
off, in a salute which served as a signal to the welcoming party to
prepare themselves. At Whitehall Stairs the young elector landed,
and was met by a deputation headed by Prince Charles, who conducted him to the Banqueting House. There, beneath Inigo Jones's
lofty pillared ceiling, the Elector Palatine saw for the first time the
princess who was to be his wife.

As Frederick approached, the English royal family saw a dark-
haired, dark-eyed boy of medium height, not outstandingly handsome, but well-built and pleasant-faced. Frederick appeared admir-
ably self-possessed: 'his approach, gesture and countenance were
seasoned with a well-becoming confidence' as he bowed low before
the king. Queen Anne was less than welcoming in her reception of
her daughter's Protestant bridegroom; she 'entertained him with a

fixed countenance', which discouraged him from attempting to do more than kiss her hand. Prince Henry, by contrast, was all friendliness. He and the visitor exchanged 'after a more familiar strain certain passages of courtesy', and then it was the turn of the Princess Elizabeth. She had been careful not to betray an immodest curiosity by appearing to look too hard at Frederick, and he too showed the strictest regard for propriety, 'stooping to take up the lowest part of her garment to kiss it'. In the most graceful fashion Elizabeth forestalled him, 'curtseying lower than accustomed, and with her hand staying him from that humblest reverence'. Instead, he kissed her. On the following day the elector revisited the king, the queen and Prince Henry, and twice Princess Elizabeth; once in the afternoon at her own lodging, in state, and after supper with somewhat less ceremony. The first meeting of the betrothed couple had been a success.

Excellent reports of the young elector began to circulate. He was judged 'straight and well-shaped for his growing years', and said to have 'a countenance pleasing, and promising both wit, courage and judgement'. The king had promptly presented him with a ring worth £1,800, and he was said to be very well liked by everybody. He was lodged at Essex House, on the west side of Temple Bar, but apartments near those of Prince Henry, in St James's Palace, were put at his disposal, as were rooms in Whitehall, and he was seen at court every day. 'The King is much pleased in him, and so is all the court,' was the general verdict.

For his part, Frederick was clearly enchanted with Elizabeth. He was said to show no interest in 'running at the ring nor tennis, nor riding with the Prince, as Count Henry his uncle and others of his company do; but only in her conversation'. His opulent new surroundings held no charms for him unless Elizabeth was present. Fortunately he was able to see her frequently, 'and they meet often at meals', it was reported.

The young Palsgrave, as he was known in England, fitted in well with English life and customs. There was every sign of a firm friendship growing up between him and Prince Henry, and from the moment of his arrival he was made welcome by the citizens of London. On 29 October, less than two weeks after his landing on English soil, he was invited to dine at the Guildhall, for the Lord Mayor's Feast; at the end of the banquet he was presented, on behalf of the City of London, with 'a very large basin and ewer of silver, richly gilded and curiously wrought; and two great gilded livery pots', valued at £500. The elector behaved with the utmost courtesy and charm, and made a point of going 'to see and salute the Lady Mayoress and her train where she sat'. The evening was not without its disappointments, however. 'Great winds on the water' almost spoiled the Lord Mayor's Show, causing several of the city companies' barges to turn back for fear of running aground, so that the newly installed Lord Mayor arrived at Westminster almost unescorted. And there was another mishap: Prince Henry, who was to have accompanied his future brother-in-law to the feast, was unwell and could not be present.

Since Frederick's first appearance at court there had been speculation about the date of the royal wedding. Some thought it would take place at Easter, 1613; in the meantime there was to be a ceaseless round of festivities, 'masques, tilts and barriers' and every sort of amusement that the Jacobean court could devise. Before the Christmas of 1612, however, an event took place which entirely overshadowed the marriage celebrations. It was a tragedy which was to have far-reaching effects, not only for Elizabeth Stuart, but for the course of seventeenth-century English history.

Prince Henry had for some time been complaining of headaches and a feeling of lassitude; he seemed low in spirits, and looked pale and thinner than usual. Early in October he had two slight fits of an ague, followed by a bout of diarrhoea, and it was thought that he had caught a chill. He was, however, determined to be up and about when the Palatine arrived, and so 'To St James's he came, seeming well, but that he looked pale and ill'. In spite of his state of health he was 'wonderfully busy in providing, and giving order for everything belonging to his care for his Sister's marriage, advancing the same by all means possible, keeping also his Highness the Palsgrave company, so much as he conveniently could'. It was a noble effort, which successfully deceived most of the Court as to his true state of health. On Saturday, 24 October, however, he overdid his efforts to appear perfectly fit; 'as though his body had been of brass', he stripped down to his shirt and played a strenuous game of tennis, just as if it had been a hot summer's day. That night his headache and drowsiness grew worse. On the following day, 'for all his great courage and strife to over-master the greatness of his evil, dissembling the same', he was overcome by sickness and fever, and was forced to go home to his bed, where he lay in severe pain, tortured with thirst. The Prince of Wales, Elizabeth's dearly-loved brother and the English people's hero, had typhoid fever.

He continued to struggle against his sickness, getting up to play cards with Prince Charles and Prince Henry of Nassau two days running, so that still no one guessed the truth about his condition. A great physician, sent for from Cambridge, confessed that he 'did not well like of the same', and by the fifth day of the prince's illness hopes began to diminish a little, but bleeding seemed to yield good results, and on 1 November he was well enough to receive a visit from the king, the queen, Prince Charles, Princess Elizabeth and the young elector all together, 'all which conceiving good hopes departed from thence reasonably cheerful'. The royal party's optimism was misplaced. Possibly it was their intention to cheer one another up; or perhaps none of the family could bear to face the truth.

The prince's condition thereafter deteriorated rapidly. He became delirious, calling for his clothes and his rapier, and shouting that 'he must be gone, he would not stay', to the great distress of those around him. Outlandish remedies were tried; his dark blond hair was shaved off, and pigeons and cupping glasses applied, in an attempt to relieve his appalling headache, and a cockerel was cut down the back and laid against the soles of his feet, 'but in vain'. For his soul's health the Archbishop of Canterbury came to see him, and ordered prayers to be said in the chamber.

On 5 November, exactly eight years after the gunpowder plotters had planned to blow up the prince with his father in the Parliament

House, word was sent to King James that his heir was dying – 'there now remained no hopes or means of his Highness's recovery'. In his despair James gave carte blanche to his personal physician, Dr Mayerne, to do whatever he chose to help the prince, without consulting the other doctors about him, but Mayerne, knowing the situation to be critical, refused to act alone, 'saying, it should never be said in after ages that he had killed the King's eldest son'. King James 'more like a dead than a living man', removed to Theobalds to await the final tragic news.

Not until that fateful 5 November was it publicly known that the prince's life was in danger. The people were appalled; when, on the following day, it was rumoured that he had already died, 'there arose wonderful great shouting, weeping and crying in the chamber, court and adjoining streets'. Remedies were sent in from many quarters; one, which was actually tried, arrived from Sir Walter Raleigh in the Tower. The brewing of this cordial, which Raleigh declared could not fail to cure the prince unless his sickness was the result of poison, was the great scholar's last act of gratitude to his young royal patron. It seemed briefly to have a good effect, for soon after taking it Prince Henry broke into a slight sweat. But nothing could save him now. The shipwright Phineas Pett arrived at St James's to find 'a house turned to the very map of true sorrow, every man with the character of grief written in his dejected countenance, all places flowing with tears and bitter lamentations'. Shortly before eight o'clock in the evening of 6 November 1612, Prince Henry died, and was 'attended into Heaven with as many prayers, tears and strong cries as ever soul was'.

The nation mourned and the king and queen were heartbroken, but no one was more stricken with grief than the dead boy's sister. 'The Lady Elizabeth is much afflicted with this loss, and not without good cause, for he did much affect her,' ran a contemporary letter. Several times during his illness Elizabeth had come to St James's in disguise to visit Henry, but each time she had been turned away before she could reach his chamber. In between his ravings the prince had asked for her, and it was said that his last coherent words were,

'Where is my dear sister?' Since her infancy Elizabeth had idolized her handsome, talented elder brother; now, in what should have been a time of intense happiness for her, he had suddenly been taken from her. The brother and sister had made a pact that her marriage should not divide them – Henry had been planning to accompany Elizabeth to her new home, and choose himself a German bride. Now she and her bridegroom would make that journey without him.

For the young and inexperienced Frederick it was a testing time. The Venetian ambassador reported that he was 'quite upset at finding himself here at such an unpropitious and lamentable juncture', but he did all he could to comfort his future wife and her mourning family. King James, who had taken his heir's death very badly, evidently found some consolation in the company of his future son-in-law. When James left Theobalds for Kensington, Frederick went with Prince Charles and Princess Elizabeth, all together in one coach, to visit him in his distress, and when the king removed to Hertfordshire ten days later he took the Elector Palatine with him.

While he was comforting the royal family, Frederick had some reason to be troubled on his own behalf. Now that the Prince of Wales was dead, only the delicate, undergrown Prince Charles stood between Elizabeth Stuart and the throne of England. It seemed possible that the gunpowder plotters' intentions of making her Queen Elizabeth II might, after all, be realized, and there were some who said that a more powerful husband than the Elector Palatine should be found for the Princess who might one day become Queen of England. The Scots in particular were said to 'take no great joy in the match', and would have preferred to see the Marquis of Hamilton, now third in line to their throne, become Elizabeth's consort.

King James, however, made it plain that he intended to proceed with the Palatine marriage. The death of the militant Protestant Prince Henry had confirmed the young elector in his position as the hope of the anti-Habsburg forces in Europe, and this was still the alliance which James required for his only daughter. In time, Prince Charles might redress the balance of English influence abroad by marrying a Spanish bride, but James's immediate concern was to confirm his unity with the Protestant powers.

'It would be thought absurd', observed a contemporary letter-writer, 'that foreign ambassadors, coming to condole the Prince's death, should find us feasting and dancing.' The marriage had to be put off until the mourning period was over, that was unavoidable; but as a sign of the king's sincerity in the business the betrothal ceremony was fixed for 27 December, scarcely three weeks after Henry's funeral.

In preparation for the great event Frederick was invested with the Order of the Garter, on 18 December. King James performed the ceremony with a marked lack of formality, in private, sitting up in his bed, as he was suffering from gout at the time. The king, 'after a few words, put the George about his neck'. Unfortunately, 'it was forgotten to have first dubbed him knight'. The ribbon and diamond star bestowed on Elizabeth's bridegroom had formerly belonged to Prince Henry.

On 27 December the Banqueting House was packed with spectators long before the ceremony was due to begin. Inigo Jones's hall had been decorated for the occasion and hung with tapestries, but mourning for the Prince of Wales had modified the customary splendour of the Jacobean court. After King James had kissed both Frederick and Elizabeth, and given them his blessing, they walked hand in hand about twenty paces into the centre of the magnificent room, to where a special Turkish carpet had been laid down for them to stand on. The young couple made a handsome sight; Frederick was dressed in purple velvet, richly laced with gold, and his cloak was lined with cloth of gold. The Princess Elizabeth looked ravishing. 'To make an even mixture of joy and mourning' she was wearing black satin with touches of silver lace, which set off her fair colouring, and she had a little plume of white feathers in her hair, a fashion which was promptly taken up by all the smart young people in London, 'which hath made white feathers dear on the sudden', it was reported.

The words of the marriage service were used for the betrothal, but instead of each responding at intervals throughout, they affirmed their vows at the end. Unfortunately Sir Thomas Lake, whose duty it was to read out the vows in French, had translated them so ineptly and spoke them with such an atrocious accent that it made everyone want to laugh, and Elizabeth and Frederick almost succumbed to a fit of giggling. Only the solemnity of the Archbishop of Canterbury, who followed Lake, restored an atmosphere of decorum, as he pronounced the words, 'The God of Abraham, Isaac and Jacob, bless these nuptials and make them prosperous to these kingdoms and to his Church'. Queen Anne, who was noted 'to have given no great grace nor favour to this match', was not present at her daughter's betrothal to the Calvinist prince; a sudden attack of gout was given as the reason for her absence.

Despite the queen's antagonism, the elector became still closer to his bride's family after the betrothal. His name was now included with those of the king's children when prayers were said for the royal family in church, and the warm friendship which had grown up between him and Prince Henry was transferred to the twelve-year-old Prince Charles. At New Year's tide Frederick was generous in his gifts to Elizabeth's family and friends; to her guardians, Lord and Lady Harington, he gave golden and gilt plate, to the value of £2,000, and he distributed £400 among their servants. To Prince Charles he gave a rapier and a pair of spurs set with diamonds, to the king an agate bottle, 'esteemed a very rare and rich jewel', and to his hostile future mother-in-law, 'a very fair cup of agate and a jewel'. His presents to Elizabeth were of a glittering magnificence – a rich diamond necklace, a diamond tiara, a pair of 'very rich' diamond earrings and two enormous pearls, 'esteemed the rarest that are to be found in Christendom'. His gifts to her alone were valued at £35,000. The 'bounty of his free gifts, presents and rewards' during his stay in England greatly added to Frederick's popularity.

The precise date of the wedding remained undecided for some time. James had proposed May Day as the earliest suitable day, with the proviso that if Frederick should be unexpectedly required in the Palatinate before then, the marriage could be celebrated immediately and Frederick could return home, leaving Elizabeth to follow him later. But the elector was anxious to marry and take his bride with him to his own country as soon as possible. Eventually an appropriate compromise was found, and 14 February, St Valentine's Day, was decided on. The Electress Louisa Juliana confirmed the arrangement in a letter to King James in which she expressed her gratitude for the English king's kindness to her son.

The tragedy of Prince Henry's death marred, but could not destroy, the young couple's happiness during the weeks that led up to their wedding. They went on boating trips to Putney, to Hampton Court and Greenwich; they rode and hunted and played cards; they sat for their portraits and they watched a succession of plays. Shakespeare's company of actors, the King's Men, received payment for 'presenting before the Princess Highness the Lady Elizabeth and the Prince Palatine Elector fourteen several plays', including *The Knot of Fools, Much Ado About Nothing, The Merry Devil of Edmonton* and *The Tempest*. The masque scene in *The Tempest*, which celebrates the betrothal of Ferdinand and Miranda, may have been specially written in honour of the royal bride and bridegroom.

The preparations for Elizabeth's wedding were well under way by the beginning of January; on the Sunday before Candlemas the banns were read in the chapel at Whitehall, 'and next Sunday is the last time of asking', wrote Mr Chamberlain, a resident of London who took a keen interest in the proceedings. He went on to describe the extraordinary preparations for festivities and shows that were under way, adding that in his opinion the fireworks and shows on the river must be costing the king £5,000 or more. Then he informed his correspondent that he had recently been at Court, and had seen both Frederick and Elizabeth. 'I had my full view of them both,' he wrote, 'but will not tell you all I think, but only this, that he owes his mistress nothing, if he were a King's son as she is a King's daughter. The worst is, methinks, he is much too young and small-timbered to undertake such a task.'

On February 7 the elector was publicly installed as a member of the Order of the Garter in St George's Chapel, Windsor. After his ceremonial investiture with Prince Henry's own insignia, the elector was proclaimed by his full titles as 'The High and Mighty Prince Frederick, by the Grace of God, Count Palatine of the Rhine, Arch-Sewer of the Holy Roman Empire, Duke of Bavaria, and Knight of the Most Noble Order of the Garter'. On the royal family's return from Windsor, Elizabeth took up residence in Prince Henry's former rooms in St James's Palace, which had been spring-cleaned and re-decorated for her use. From Frederick's Garter insignia to Elizabeth's lodgings, the betrothed couple had constant reminders of 'our dead, dear and never to be forgotten Prince Henry', to cast a shadow over their wedding preparations.

The poets and balladmongers who poured out verses in celebration of the Princess Elizabeth's marriage constantly referred to the royal tragedy while expressing their joy in the royal festivities.

> Heaven the first hath thrown away
> Her weary weed of mourning hue
> And waits Eliza's wedding-day
> In starry-spangled gown of blue,

proclaimed one, while another wrote charmingly,

> There is great strife 'twixt death and love
> Which of them is the stronger
> And which of them can strike the stroke
> Whose wound endures the longer,

concluding with the lines,

> We know love is as strong as Death
> But Death to Love must yield,
> For Death is past, Love still remains,
> God Cupid wins the field.

'The marriage draws near, and all things are ready,' it was reported on 11 February. 'On Sunday was their last time of asking openly in the Chapel.' Queen Anne had at last become reconciled to the prospect of a Protestant son-in-law, and appeared to have become very fond of Frederick. 'The Queen grows every day more favourable,' ran a contemporary letter, 'and there is hope that she will grace [the marriage] with her presence.'

The evening of 11 February saw the first of the elaborate entertainments performed upon the Thames. The river had been transformed for the occasion; 'great pinnaces, galleys, galliasses, carricks, with great store of other smaller vessels' floated at anchor above London Bridge, while on the bank opposite Whitehall the town of Algiers had magically sprung up, ready to be bombarded from the water for the spectators' delight. The first night's festivities centred round a magnificent display of fireworks. As the Princess Elizabeth, the elector and the rest of the royal family stood marvelling at a window of the palace, the stars above them were 'hoodwinked with the burning exhalations'. To the thunder of cannon positioned in the nearby fields, a shining dragon sprang into the air, 'against which another fiery vision appeared, flaming like to St George on horseback'. The apparitions battled together until the dragon, vanquished, exploded with a roar and disappeared, 'but the Champion, with his flaming horse, for a little time made a show of triumphant conquest, and so ceased'. Then came a scene after the young couple's own hearts – a 'fiery hunting'. All in fireworks, a pack of hounds came chasing across the sky, in pursuit of a hart, 'making many rebounds and turns with much strangeness, skipping upon the air as if it had been a usual hunting upon land'. When the fire and smoke cleared from this display, a fleet of ships and galleys 'bravely rigged with top and top-gallant, with their flags and streamers waving like men of war' came sailing into view, and proceeded to perform a marvellous sea-fight among the stars. As the contemporary chronicler of the display observed, 'when Kings' commands be, art is stretched to the true depth'. The fireworks for the elector and princess were a triumph of Jacobean artifice.

On the following day the king ordered a general rest from these spectacular entertainments, both as a respite and to allow time for preparation for the next day's show, 'which moved a more longing desire in the hearts of his subjects to see the same'. Their hopes of a yet more entrancing entertainment were not fulfilled, however.

The events of Saturday, 13 February began promisingly enough. Between two and three o'clock in the afternoon the king and his family 'placed themselves in great royalty upon the privy stairs of Whitehall' and saw a Venetian man-of-war and a caravel come sailing up to do battle with seventeen Turkish galleys, 'which lay hovering upon Lambeth side'. A barrier of barges chained together had been strung across the Thames to prevent over-eager spectators in boats from approaching too closely to the mock-fight, which culminated in the arrival of a fleet of fifteen English pinnaces, flying the red cross of St George, 'to the great delight of all the beholders, which as then seemed to cover over the Thames in boats and barges'. Ultimately the Turks were forced to yield to the English admiral, who brought his prisoners-of-war under guard to the royal onlookers at the Privy Stairs. The entertainment was marred by some tragic accidents, however : in the simulated battling one man was blinded, another lost his hands, and several more were injured. The shipwright Phineas Pett, who had been persuaded against his inclinations to serve as captain of a sixty-ton pinnace, found that in this 'jesting business' he 'ran more danger than if it had been a sea service in good earnest'.

As a climax to the day's amusements a large number of guns were shot off in St George's Fields. The noise was so loud, and lasted so long, that the hearers were astonished. 'Thus ended Saturday's shows upon the waters, being the eve of this great Marriage-day.'

Elizabeth Stuart's wedding was as magnificent as the elaborate festivities that had preceded it. One of those who had a good view of the princess as she passed by in her bridal robes wrote : 'The excess of bravery, and the continued succession of new company, did so dazzle me, that I could not observe the tenth part of what I wished.' The ceremony took place in the chapel of Whitehall Palace, but Elizabeth's bridal procession arrived by a long route so that as many people as possible might see her. As a sign of virginity her long golden hair hung down loose, almost to her waist, and between every strand was woven 'a roll or list of gold-spangles, pearls, rich stones and diamonds'. On her head was a gold coronet, 'exceeding rich', which King James announced to be worth a million crowns, and which was thickly set with diamonds and pearls. Her dress was of cloth of silver, richly embroidered with silver, according to Mr Chamberlain, and its sleeves were sewn with many more diamonds, which 'dazzled and amazed the eyes of the beholders'. The sixteen-year-old princess must have seemed a fairy-tale figure as she moved slowly towards the chapel, surrounded by her ladies, 'attired in white satin gowns, adorned with many rich jewels'. Her bridesmaids were poetically described as 'a sky of celestial stars', attending on 'fair Phoebe'. Lord and Lady Harington both walked near her in the procession, while the king and queen followed behind. In Mr Chamberlain's opinion they cut less impressive figures than most: 'The King, methought, was somewhat strangely attired in a cap and feather, with a Spanish cape and a long stocking.' Queen Anne was dressed all in white, 'but not very rich, saving in jewels'. James did, however, have a diamond in his hat which was judged to be 'of wonderful great value'.

The chapel had been 'in royal sort adorned' for the great occasion. It was decorated with hangings depicting the Acts of the Apostles, and the Communion table was covered with plate of great value. In the middle of the chapel a scaffold had been erected, about five feet high and twenty feet wide, to which the bridal party mounted by six or seven stairs. The king, Prince Charles, Prince Frederick and Prince Henry of Nassau took their places on one side; the queen sat on the other, with the bride herself, who was seated on a stool, her train supported by Lady Harington.

After the Gentlemen of the Chapel had sung an anthem, the Bishop of Bath and Wells preached a sermon on the predictable subject of the marriage at Cana of Galilee, which lasted for about half an hour. Then the choir sang another anthem, from the psalm 'Blessed art thou that fearest God', and after that Elizabeth and Frederick stood together for the marriage service. Frederick, who was resplendent in a suit of silver, with the diamond George that Elizabeth had given him glittering on his breast, had 'learned as much as concerned his part reasonably perfect', and the service was conducted entirely in English, although French was the language which Frederick and Elizabeth normally spoke to one another. They were married 'in all points according to the Book of Common Prayer', and King James gave his daughter away. Elizabeth herself showed no signs of being either nervous or tearful, but was clearly glowing with happiness; at one moment her customary high spirits threatened to overcome her sense of dignity. As one account discreetly phrased it: 'While the Archbishop of Canterbury was solemnizing the Marriage, some Coruscations and Lightnings of Joy appeared in her Countenance that Expressed more than an ordinary smile, being almost elated to a Laughter.'

There could be no doubt that Elizabeth Stuart was a happy bride. The marriage arranged for reasons of state had turned out to be a love-match, and the two young people brought together by religion and politics had formed a relationship which was to prove deep and enduring. They were of the same age, they were healthy and good-looking and their mutual passion for horses and hunting was only one of the tastes which they had in common. Frederick had entered Elizabeth's life at a fortunate moment; his presence had served to soften the blow of her adored brother's death, and sorrow had strengthened their dependence on one another from the outset. In some respects the beautiful Elizabeth lacked emotional warmth; she freely admitted that she did not like children, and among her own sons and daughters she was to show shameless favouritism. But her love for her husband was never in doubt, and on her wedding-day her joy was evident to all.

When the marriage service was over, the new husband and wife were proclaimed by Garter King at Arms. 'All health, happiness and honour be to the high and mighty Prince, Frederick the Fifth,' he announced, 'and to Elizabeth his wife, only daughter of the high, mighty and right-excellent James, by the grace of God, King of Great Britain.' Less stylized congratulations followed, as the newly married couple were toasted with bowls of wine and hippocras brought from the vestry. 'An health was begun to the prosperity of the marriage out of a great gold bowl by the Prince Palatine and answered by the Princess and others present, in their order.' Then, 'with great joy', the company returned to the Banqueting House.

Elizabeth was led back by the Duke of Lennox and the Earl of Nottingham, while Frederick was preceded by six of his German entourage, dressed in crimson velvet encrusted with gold lace, carrying six silver trumpets, 'who no sooner coming into the Banqueting House, but they presented him with a melodious sound of the same'. Outside the crowds sent back a roar of 'God give them joy, God give them joy!' That evening the Elector Palatine and his new electress dined in state in the Banqueting House, and the 'dancing, masking and revelling' continued into the night.

> Scatter nuts without the door
> The married is a child no more
> For whosoe'er a wife hath wed
> Hath other business in his head,

declared one of the hundreds of verses celebrating the marriage of 'Beauty's mirror, fair Elizabeth'.

> Likewise Eliza goes to breed and bring
> Forth to the light, sons of a noble kind,
> Whose worth one day shall make us Britons sing,

ran another. Jacobean frankness, rather than literary merit, was the chief virtue of most of the poems written for the occasion. John Donne's 'Epithalamium' on 'The Lady Elizabeth and Count Palatine being married on St Valentine's Day' had greater claims to poetic excellence, however. It concluded with the charming stanza,

> And by the act of these two Phoenixes
>   Nature again restored is
>   For since these two are two no more
> There's but one Phoenix still, as was before.
>   Rest now at last, and we
>   As Satyrs watch the sun's uprise, will stay
> Waiting, when your eyes opened let out day
> Only desired, because your face we see;

Others near you shall whispering speak
And wagers lay, at which side day will break,
And win by observing, then, whose hand it is
That opens first a curtain, hers or his;
This will be tried tomorrow after nine,
Till which hour, we thy day enlarge, O Valentine.

On the morning after their wedding Elizabeth and Frederick received a call from King James, who came 'to visit these young turtles that were coupled on St Valentine's Day'. With his customary prurience he proceeded to put some intimate questions to his new son-in-law concerning the events of the past night, and was sufficiently assured that the marriage had indeed been consummated. That afternoon the king, Prince Charles and the elector took part in some courtly sports, running at the ring, and then the elector had an opportunity to show off his horsemanship, 'mounted on a high-bounding horse, which he managed so like a horseman that he was exceedingly commended'. Elizabeth, with her mother and their ladies, watched her new husband's display from a window of the Banqueting House.

That evening it was the turn of the Middle Temple and Lincoln's Inn to present a masque. Designed by Inigo Jones and written by George Chapman, the entertainment was a resounding success. The performers and their assistants set out for St James's Palace from the house of the Master of the Rolls, and they provided 'a gallant and glorious show' as they made their way up Fleet Street and along the Strand. Gentlemen on horseback with their attendants were followed by a dozen capering little boys dressed as baboons; after them came two fantastically decorated triumphal chariots, bearing musicians, and then a group of Red Indians. The spectators judged it 'the best show that hath been seen many a day'. King James, watching from a gallery at Whitehall, ordered them to make a circuit of the tiltyard, and then they proceeded through St James's Park to their destination. The king was delighted with the show, and let it be known that he 'never saw so many proper men together'. He made a point of seeing that the masquers were well looked after at the banquet that followed, and the Master of the Rolls and his fellow-organizer were rewarded with royal pats and caresses.

On the following day Gray's Inn and the Inner Temple were due to present their masque, but their efforts met with less success. Since their rivals had arrived on horses and in chariots, through the streets, they decided that they would come by water, all the way from Southwark, 'which suited well with their device, which was the marriage of the river of Thames to the Rhine'. The evening's pleasures began with a charming sight: 'infinite store of lights, very curiously set and placed' twinkled through the darkness, as the boats and barges, decked with lamps and lights, came gliding up the river. The onlookers were enchanted with the scene, and by the time the masquers landed at the Privy Stairs it was generally expected that they would outdo the previous night's show. The journey by water had cost at least three hundred pounds, 'and great expectation there was that they should every way excel their competitors that went before them'. But they were to be disappointed. The masque never took place. The great hall was too full to be cleared for them; many of the court ladies, having made their way to the galleries to watch the barges coming up the river, could not get back into the hall; and most dampening of all, the king was so exhausted by the revelry of the two previous nights that he had no inclination to see yet another elaborate entertainment. When Sir Francis Bacon, the organizer of the 'Marriage of Thames and Rhine', pleaded with James not to forgo the performance, and, 'as it were, bury them quick', the king answered wittily 'that then they must bury him quick, for he could last no longer'. He spoke kindly to the crestfallen masquers, and invited them to return on the following Saturday. But the fun had gone out of the plan. The costumes had now been seen by everyone, and the vital element of surprise would be missing. In any case, another play had already been arranged for Saturday.

As it turned out, however, the newly married couple were able to see both productions on the following Saturday, and the 'Marriage of Thames and Rhine' was received with loud applause and approval.

The king was very pleased with Bacon's production, and showed his satisfaction by inviting the masquers and their assistants to dine with him on the following night. The cost of this supper was borne by the elector and some of his companions, who tactfully lost it to the king upon a wager of running at the ring.

Though James was spared the price of that dinner, his expenditure for the wedding of his only daughter had been enormous. More than £50,000 had been lavished on the round of fireworks, feasts and festivities, and he had yet to find the £40,000 for the bride's portion. It had been a magnificent display, but when it was over and the reckoning came, James found himself badly out of pocket. Lord Harington, too, found that the Princess Elizabeth's marriage had cost him dear: having had the responsibility for ordering her trousseau he had been obliged to spend more than £3,500 of his own money. Unable to repay him in cash, the king granted him a patent which gave him the right to coin brass farthings, known thereafter as 'Haringtons'. For his own part, James had to cut down his expenses and he began by summarily dismissing his new son-in-law's attendants who had been receiving his hospitality. It was a decision which greatly upset Elizabeth, and it effectively marked the end of the hectic round of celebrations. Two days after the performance of the 'Marriage of Thames and Rhine', the king left town.

'We are now preparing for the Lady Elizabeth's departure,' Mr Chamberlain wrote on 14 March, one month after the wedding. 'I am of opinion her train will not be so great by many degrees as was expected, for we devise all the means we can to cut off expense, and not without cause.' With his household being broken up Frederick was increasingly anxious to return home to Heidelberg with his bride, but King James seemed reluctant to appoint an early date for his only daughter's departure. 'The number and quality of her attendants vary each day,' reported Chamberlain. 'The time of her departure varies likewise in common report, being, they say, put off from 8 April until after St George's Day, that they may have fair moonlight nights at sea.'

Frederick and Elizabeth were briefly separated when the young bridegroom went to join the king at Newmarket. On 6 March he and Prince Charles visited Cambridge, where they were obliged to sit through two over-long comedies. A similar invitation to visit Oxford was courteously declined on the grounds of lack of time; the sixteen-year-old husband and wife clearly disliked being parted from one another.

After Frederick's return to London the last phase of entertainments and excursions was entered upon. A grand tilting on 23 March, the anniversary of King James's accession to the English throne, was followed by an expedition to the Tower of London the next day. A salute was fired in honour of the royal visit; Elizabeth, with her usual pluck and high spirits, took the match from one of the gunners and set off the cannon herself.

'The marriage consummated, and these royalties ended', the time had come for the Count Palatine of the Rhine and the 'lovely nymph of stately Thames' to leave England. On Saturday, 10 April, three weeks after Elizabeth had lit the fuse of a gun at the Tower, another salute was fired in her honour from those same cannon, as, with her husband, her parents, and her brother she was rowed down the river from Whitehall towards Greenwich. Half a century was to pass before Elizabeth Stuart would see London and the Thames again.

As the royal barges left Whitehall, huge crowds lined the river banks to watch the princess's departure. 'All well-affected people take great pleasure and contentment in this match,' Chamberlain had written. Elizabeth's marriage had served to confirm and increase her already great popularity with her father's subjects, and she was now firmly established as the darling of the Protestant English. As they glided past the cheering crowds on that spring day in 1613, the future looked bright for Elizabeth and Frederick.

CHAPTER FOUR
The Electress

'I shall perhaps never see again the flower of princes, the King of fathers, the best and most amiable father that the sun will ever see,' Elizabeth wrote woefully on 16 April 1613. She and her husband were staying at the Deanery, in Canterbury, while they waited for a favourable wind; two days earlier they had said farewell to King James and Queen Anne. Prince Charles had remained with the newly-married couple, intending to see them embark, but her brother's presence did not prevent Elizabeth from missing her parents. Her heart was 'pressed and astounded', she wrote, and she longed to return again to her father to kiss his hands once more.

On 21 April the elector and his new electress travelled to Margate, and there they were rowed out to where the *Prince Royal* lay at anchor. Since the day when Elizabeth and the royal family had gone to see her launched and been disappointed, the great ship named after Prince Henry had been attended by mishaps; as the shipwright Phineas Pett recounted, there were some, such as Lord Northampton, who would have preferred the Princess Elizabeth 'not to venture her person in such a vessel that had so ill a beginning'. She was not to be dissuaded by such talk, however, and she and Frederick were duly received on board by the Lord Admiral. Lord and Lady Harington and their personal attendants accompanied them onto the man-of-war, and hundreds more retainers took their places in the fleet of smaller ships which were to sail with them to Flushing. Everything was made ready, but 'the wind getting easterly, and likely to be foul weather, her Highness and the Palsgrave and most part of her train were carried ashore'. They were obliged to spend the next three nights in Margate, and it was not until 25 April that they found themselves under way at last. On 28 April, after a 'short and prosperous passage over the seas', the Elector and Electress Palatine cast anchor before Flushing.

Frederick's uncle and guardian, Prince Maurice of Orange, was there to welcome them. He went out to the little fleet, and not only gave the new arrivals formal greeting, but stayed for supper and spent the night on board the *Prince Royal*. On the following day Elizabeth stepped onto foreign soil for the first time in her life. A barge decorated with crimson velvet and manned by twenty English rowers, who kept time to a band of musicians playing in the stern, brought her to shore, and from there, amidst a rapturous welcome from the Dutch citizens, she insisted on making her way on foot through the streets to her lodging. It was a novel and highly effective gesture for a royal personage to walk amongst the cheering crowds; it was a touch of which her godmother Queen Elizabeth I might have approved.

A parting followed. Frederick was not only the King of England's son-in-law: he was the prince of an important state, and now that he had returned to the Continent he had the duties of government to perform again. On 30 April he left his wife's side and hurried to The Hague, where he was needed to endorse a treaty that was being signed between the German princes of the Protestant Union, of whom he was the head, and the States-General of the United Provinces. Elizabeth travelled on without him, accompanied by the Lord High Admiral of England, as well as the Princes Maurice and Henry. At Middleburgh, where she spent three days, she received 'royal and hearty entertainment' and was magnificently feasted.

At the beginning of April the Lord High Admiral and Phineas Pett had left for England. The admiral took with him a letter from the electress to her father; after commending the bearer for his extraordinary favours and courtesies, Elizabeth wrote: 'The admiral will declare to your majesty the love of all the people of this country and the honour that I received.' Her first impressions of her new life had been favourable.

At Rotterdam, which the royal party reached on 5 May, Frederick rejoined his wife, bringing with him the English ambassador at The Hague, Sir Ralph Winwood, and a cousin of Elizabeth's, Sophia Hedwig of Brunswick, whose Danish mother was the sister of Queen Anne. The blonde, good-natured Sophia wished to be the first Princess of Holland to greet the illustrious new arrival, and the two young women took a great liking to each other.

From Rotterdam they proceeded to the pretty old town of Delft, and from Delft to The Hague, where Prince Maurice of Orange formally received Elizabeth at the head of a troop of horse. 'Nothing was wanting that was in the invention of man held fit to give content-ment to such Princely Guests' during their stay, and they spent five happy days 'in hunting, in plays and other costly shows', before Frederick left Elizabeth's side and hurried on to Heidelberg to superintend the arrangements for his wife's reception. During one triumphant hunt Elizabeth herself shot down three stags. On her departure the States-General presented her with magnificent gifts.

In Amsterdam, which she reached by boat on 13 May, she was greeted with a volley of six hundred great shot, sent from two ships, and presented with another immensely valuable present consisting of gold plate. Then she left Holland, departing from Amsterdam to Utrecht. In Utrecht she had the pleasing experience of mounting the Cathedral tower, over three hundred feet high, and gazing out over the cities of Holland on an ideally clear afternoon. Sightseeing, hunt-ing and banqueting were the order of the day wherever she went.

A less welcome gesture of friendship was offered by the Archduke Albert and his wife, Isabella of Spain, Governors of the Spanish Netherlands, who sent letters inviting Elizabeth to stay at their castle on her way through their town of Rheinbeck. Coming from such avowed enemies of the Protestant cause the offer was highly suspect. To refuse would be offensive, but to accept might well be dangerous; it was decided that the answer must be a courteous negative. In contrast, the hospitality offered by the young Margrave of Brandenburg was delightful; he entertained Elizabeth to a picnic in the open fields near the little village of Mondorf.

A ship specially ordered for the new electress's journey conveyed her up the Rhine at the end of May. Beautifully designed and lavishly fitted, the ship had a crowned lion on the bows and, equally appropriate for Elizabeth Stuart, the figure of Fortune delicately poised on the stern. The early summer was a pleasant time for a journey up the Rhine toward the Palatinate, with frequent stops along the route. It was also, however, the season for the plague, and messengers arrived from Frederick to warn Elizabeth that several towns along the way were infected, and that she must not land in any of those areas.

Bacharach, which had been named in the marriage contract as the point at which the King of England was to cease to pay his daughter's expenses, was one of the places which she passed without stopping. Soon after, a small craft was seen coming up river towards her ship; to Elizabeth's delight, Frederick was on board. That night they dined together for the first time in the Palatinate, in the village of Gaulheim.

The enthusiastic welcome which Elizabeth had been receiving at every stage of her journey was redoubled in her own new country. She found that such popularity had one notable drawback: the necessity for distributing presents as she passed through cities and towns had left her without the means to give tokens of good will, and she was obliged to pledge an item of value to her jeweller in order to obtain the resources to maintain the diplomatic custom. Pawning her valuables was an indignity with which she was to become all too familiar in later years.

At Frankenthal, one of Elizabeth's dower towns where it had been agreed in her marriage articles that she should be granted a residence, she was 'joyfully received with an infinite concourse of people' and greeted by the local burghers, dressed as Turks, Poles and 'Switzers', who conducted the party to their lodgings in a stately procession. The next night there was a magnificent pageant depicting the Siege of Troy and on the following day Elizabeth proceeded on her own to Heidelberg, without her husband. Frederick had gone ahead so that he might welcome her formally to her new home.

The burgers of the town with all expressions of love, joy and duty, received her with hearty welcomes, the windows of every house being filled with men, women and children of all degrees; and the streets covered with throngs of people, drawn thither by the fame of such shows and pageants as were builded to add honour to this entertainment, but especially to behold her upon whom all their eyes were fixed with love and admiration.

Elizabeth's entry into Heidelberg on Monday 7 June, was triumphal. She was welcomed outside the city by her husband, and then, with Frederick riding ahead of her, she was carried in a scarlet velvet-lined coach drawn by six horses across the river Neckar. The first pageant of the day was presented by local fishermen as the procession crossed the bridge; Frederick sent the humble performers wine with which to drink the health of his bride. A series of ornamental arches were passed under; guns roared out salutes; the people waved and cheered and Elizabeth smiled with happiness as her coach rumbled through the crowded streets. The University of Heidelberg had put up four decorated arches in all, and under the second the Rector stood ready to welcome the illustrious new arrival with a lengthy speech in Latin, to which Colonel Schomberg replied on Elizabeth's behalf. A small boy then stepped forward and produced an even more acceptable offering: in the name of the goddesses Flora and Pomona he handed up a basket of luscious fruit. As the coach rolled on, the beautiful new electress was seen to possess a healthy sixteen-year-old's appetite.

In the courtyard of Heidelberg Castle the most elaborate arch of all had been built; standing more than sixty-five feet high, it supported statues which illustrated previous marriage alliances between the Palatinate and England. It was early evening when Elizabeth's carriage passed under it and drew up before the castle. Frederick dismounted and went to help his wife down before presenting her to his mother, who stood waiting to greet her.

The daughter of William the Silent received the daughter of James I with every sign of affection. Louisa Juliana embraced her daughter-in-law fondly. After a journey lasting six weeks, the Electress Palatine had finally arrived in her new home.

Heidelberg Castle was an impressive residence even for a princess accustomed to the beauties of Whitehall, St James's Palace and Hampton Court. Built of reddish-coloured local stone and ornamented with statues, it had an extraordinarily fine view northwards over mountains and woods. The Neckar flowed through the foreground and the Rhine wound its way across the far distance. Elizabeth must often have walked or sat on the great stone balcony which looked out over the huddled houses of Heidelberg towards the horizons of her husband's country. As a contemporary writer assured loyal Englishmen concerned for their princess's well-being in her new home: 'The land is very fruitful of wine, corn and other comfortable fruits for man's use, having the Rhine and Neckar running through it.' The same writer observed: 'His Highness's country is neither so small, unfruitful or mean as is by some supposed. It is in length about 200 English miles, the Lower and Upper Country. In the Lower the Prince hath twenty-six walled towns, besides an infinite number of good and fair villages.'

Frederick's father, who had ruled the Palatinate as the Elector Frederick IV from 1583 until his death in 1610, had done much to re-establish his country's influence in Germany, in both religious and cultural affairs. The original Pfalzgraf, or Count Palatine, had been the emperor's closest aide; since that role was no longer open to the Protestant Palsgraves, Frederick cast himself instead in the role of leader of Protestant influence in Germany. In May 1608, along with eight other princes and the leaders of seventeen imperial cities, he concluded the defensive pact known as the Union. He was its director; general of the war council was his indefatigable minister Christian of Anhalt, who succeeded in securing for the Union the valuable support of King Henry IV of France. Though the Union was countered in the following year by the formation of a Catholic League headed by Maximilian of Bavaria, and it was from the first weakened by the disunity between its Lutheran and Calvinist members, the role of leader of the Union of Protestant Princes nevertheless added greatly to the Elector Palatine's prestige.

Religion was the driving motivation behind Frederick iv's life and actions, but he had other interests. Though not himself a noted intellectual such as King James i of England, he took a keen interest in learning, and under him Heidelberg University became a lively centre of scholarship. His other main preoccupation had less fortunate results: he enjoyed too well the fine wines produced by his fertile lands, and the alcoholism to which he succumbed did much to hasten his death at the age of thirty-six.

To Elizabeth's delight, the Palatinate was as rich in game as it was in vineyards, and there was excellent hunting to be had. Within a week of her arrival, as a respite from thanksgiving, celebration and ceremonial, a great hunt was got up for her enjoyment, during which she shot twelve deer with her crossbow and killed a stag from the saddle. It was the first of many such happy hunting-parties. Elizabeth soon earned herself the name of 'a second Diana' from her new countrymen.

Early in July the English nobles who had accompanied her into Germany began to take their leave. Lord and Lady Harington departed after the rest; tragically, Lord Harington was destined never to see England and Combe Abbey again. At Worms he developed a fever, and he died there. Lady Harington returned to England a widow, to face huge debts incurred during their guardianship of the Princess Elizabeth.

The affection and guidance that the Haringtons had given Elizabeth during her childhood were to stand her in good stead throughout her life. In one respect, however, her upbringing had been deficient: she had reached maturity without acquiring practical experience of managing a great household. With the best of intentions, she quickly ran into difficulties when called upon, as a sixteen-

C

year-old bride, to act as mistress of Heidelberg Castle. Colonel Schomberg, who received four hundred pounds a year from James I for acting as his daughter's adviser and factotum, was driven almost to distraction by the perpetual problems of the young electress's ménage. 'Is not this a miserable life?' he wrote on one occasion.

The delicate question of precedence, which soon arose, was dealt with in accordance with the express wishes of James I; it was made known that Elizabeth Stuart must take precedence over everyone else in the Palatinate. On visits to neighbouring courts, however, such as that of the Duke of Württemberg, the King of England's insistence on his daughter's right of superiority was to prove a continuing problem.

The servant question was another source of discontent; more than a hundred English hangers-on stayed on in the town of Heidelberg after the ambassador's departure, and Elizabeth was obliged to take action to rid the town of her unwanted compatriots' presence. She drew up a list containing the names of all those who were her genuine attendants, and Schomberg arranged a passage home for the rest. 'I am doing my best to put the affairs and train of Madame into good order,' he wrote harassedly, 'but I fear that I shall not have great success.' 'Madame allows herself to be led by anyone,' was another of his complaints; 'this makes some of her attendants take upon themselves more authority than they should.'

Elizabeth's own servants refused to wait upon anyone but her, and her cupbearer insisted on his right to hand her her cup, despite the custom which decreed that at grand banquets the great nobles present should have that privilege. Such 'little dissensions' made daily life at Heidelberg very difficult for the new Electress Palatine during the summer of 1613.

All through this trying time Elizabeth was pregnant with her first child. It had been conceived before she and Frederick left England, and in her farewell letter to her father from Canterbury she had referred to her condition, but this great cause for joy was for some reason a matter which she was determined to keep secret from the world. Not only did she resolutely insist on riding and hunting as hard as ever, she appeared scarcely to admit even to herself that she really was with child. The French envoy M. de Sainte Catherine, conveying his king and queen's congratulations to the expectant mother, was surprised to receive the reply that others' belief in her condition helped her to believe in it herself. Writing to her husband's aunt, the Duchess Charlotte de la Trémoille, after the birth, Elizabeth begged to be excused the 'little dissimulation', which was, she said, to be attributed to her natural desire not to deceive the world with false hopes. 'There is nothing more repugnant to my simple disposition', she explained, 'than to give heed to appearances where I doubt the facts.' Whatever the reason for her attempted deception, the outcome was the birth of a large and healthy male child to the Elector and Electress Palatine, on Sunday 2 January 1614.

Britain rang with rejoicing when the happy news arrived. King James settled £2,000 a year on his dutiful daughter, 'as an open testimony of his love to her and delight in the birth of her son', and the baby, christened Frederick Henry in combined honour of his father, his grandfather, his great-grandfather and his late maternal uncle, was given English nationality and declared next in line to the Stuart throne after Prince Charles and Elizabeth herself. 'The Citizens of London were very joyful, and manifested the same by ringing of bells and making bonfires, on account of the birth.' The Scots were as delighted as the English. 'For joy of the news of the happy delivery of Lady Elizabeth', a mighty salute of many guns was shot off in Edinburgh, and with the aid of coals and tar barrels huge bonfires blazed out a welcome from Arthur's Seat. Elizabeth's long absence from the country of her birth had done nothing to diminish her popularity among her father's northern subjects. Prince Charles, at thirteen, was still undersized and frail; remembering the robust Prince Henry's early death, there were many who foresaw a day when a child of the Princess Elizabeth might be crowned at Westminster and rule from Whitehall.

The poetic hopes expressed at the time of Elizabeth's marriage, that she would shortly 'a joyful and glad mother prove', and that the loyal Englishmen who rejoiced at her wedding would 'live to see/A

Frederick Henry on her knee' had been most happily fulfilled. It seemed at this time as though Elizabeth Stuart had been marked out for good fortune. She and her husband were in the flower of their youth, very much in love, rulers of a peaceful and prosperous country, and now they had been blessed with a fine healthy son to safeguard the future. The christening of the first of her children, which took place on 6 March 1614, was a high point in the happiest phase of Elizabeth's life.

Chief sponsor to the child whom Elizabeth referred to as her 'little black babie' was King James of England. His presents to his first grandson were a solid gold basin and ewer. None of the godparents' gifts were, however, so tragically apt as that of Prince Maurice of Orange: his choice for the child who was to drown in a boating accident at the age of fourteen was an exquisite crystal ship.

The minor irritations of daily life at Heidelberg, trivial as they would afterwards appear in comparison with the misfortunes which were to befall her, continued to be a source of vexation to the young electress and the long-suffering Colonel Schomberg. Elizabeth Stuart was her father's daughter in matters of money; she seemed unable to reconcile her income with her expenditure, and Schomberg grew increasingly harassed as he endeavoured to instil a sense of responsibility into her. Elizabeth was weak-willed about money; according to Schomberg, she gave all she had away, not from natural generosity so much as the inability to resist 'importunities, complaints and tears'. She now had £4,500 a year from her father, and King James refused to allow her any more; had it not been for the ceaseless efforts of Schomberg, she would have run deeply into debt.

In October 1614, while 'he that hath the best hand', in Elizabeth's words, 'to set all things in a good way' was absent from the court, a serious cause for concern became apparent in the behaviour of the Elector Frederick. Having attained his majority during the summer, on his eighteenth birthday, he had attended an assembly of the Union of Protestant Princes, at Heilbronn. While there he had contracted a fever and had become very ill. Aware of the frightening memories of Prince Henry's sudden death which the news might awaken, he had insisted that his wife should not be told, and had only returned to Heidelberg when he felt better. A noticeable change had come over him, however, and he was in the grip of a depression which he seemed unable to shake off. Elizabeth was worried. In a letter to the English Secretary of State, Sir Ralph Winwood, she described her husband's low condition: 'Himself, at this late Assembly, got an ague,' she explained, 'which, though it held him not long, yet hath it made him weak and look very ill. Since his fits left him he is very heavy, and so extremely melancholy as I never saw in my life so great an alteration in any.' At this difficult moment the troublesome question of her precedence had arisen again – 'which I think they do the Prince wrong in putting into his head at this time, when he is but too melancholy', she wrote vexedly. Her mother-in-law, Louisa Juliana, was at the root of the problem; she was resentful at having to give way to the youthful new electress. Altogether it was a trying time for Elizabeth, and she badly missed the services of the absent Colonel Schomberg. 'I find none so truly careful of me as that man,' she told Winwood.

On his return to Heidelberg the colonel set to work to put Elizabeth's affairs into order. She complained that her mother-in-law wanted her to become entirely German, and to follow the customs of her new country in everything, 'which I neither have been bred to, nor is it necessary in every thing I should follow'. Schomberg forcefully reminded Frederick of the importance of the promises he had made to the King of England at the time of his departure with his bride; he had assured King James that Elizabeth's status would be carefully preserved, and that she would take precedence over all others in the Palatinate. It was unfortunate that the dowager electress should be 'envious that Madame should enjoy a different entertainment from herself', but it was unavoidable.

Where Elizabeth's own failings of extravagance and weakness with her servants were concerned, Schomberg advised a similarly firm line. He drew up lengthy lists of instructions on household management, which contained much sound common sense. He advised Elizabeth to keep careful accounts of all her expenditure, and to ensure that every dress was paid for before she wore it; to put all her old dresses away in a wardrobe and examine them once a year, giving away those which she would never wear again, and the same with tapestry and furniture; he mildly reproved her for not keeping strict inventories of all her linen, pointing out that there must be some abuse somewhere since she had brought £3,000 worth with her from England and had purchased another £1,000 worth since her arrival and yet was still ill-provided; he recommended that all her jewellery and 'pretty bagatelles' should be safely locked away in her closet, with inventories. As for the problems with her servants, he directed her, among other measures, never to listen to tales, to put an end to gossip and flirtations, not to allow her indulgence to be abused, and to be generally more strict. The counsel, 'let order and reason govern Your Highness', summed up the sensible attitudes which Schomberg sought to instil into the inexperienced young mistress of Heidelberg Castle. The new domestic régime yielded good results, and soon Elizabeth's accounts no longer showed her to be out of pocket.

In the spring of 1615, Elizabeth and Frederick had a happier subject to occupy their thoughts: they were undertaking a journey into the Upper Palatinate. Five days' travelling overland divided the two portions of Frederick's country; perhaps remembering the enthusiastic welcome she had received at every stage of her journey to Heidelberg, Elizabeth was eager to visit the rest of her husband's dominions. Frederick Henry, who was growing into a very healthy and attractive child, went to stay with his grandmother, who was delighted to have him, and wrote a fondly praising letter to her fellow-grandparent the King of England. On 18 June, after a triumphant journey, the elector and electress reached the town of Amberg, 'the principal town of the said country', as Elizabeth called it in a letter to her father. The journey did Frederick good; his spirits improved, and Elizabeth was able to write: 'I hope his melancholy is so past as it will not return in that height.' In travelling up and down they passed the summer weeks happily and returned to Heidelberg on 15 August, just in time for the elector's nineteenth birthday, which he celebrated, amid great rejoicing, on the following day.

'Their Highnesses, God be thanked, are very well and love one another more than ever,' Schomberg wrote in the summer of 1615. He added the pleasing domestic detail, 'Madame is, at this moment, playing with and caressing her little prince.' Tragedy was in store for the worthy colonel, however. Within a year of his marriage, his wife Anne Dudley died in childbed on 8 December 1615. Elizabeth grieved for her, with a hint of royal egotism : 'She is a great loss to me, for she was very careful in all that concerned me,' she wrote to King James. The question of a replacement for the faithful Dudley had immediately to be considered, and the electress was anxious that her father should not be over-hasty in appointing her successor – 'I entreat you to consider that it is not every one who is fitted for it in this country and this place.'

The diplomat and poet Sir Henry Wotton, 'sent to lie abroad for his country', visited Heidelberg in the early summer of 1616, and had the opportunity to discuss this and other matters with Elizabeth. He found her very well and in blooming looks. 'My lady your daughter', he informed the King of England, 'retaineth still her former virginal verdure in her complexion and features, though she be now the mother of one of the sweetest children that I think the world can yield.' Wotton observed the behaviour of the elector and electress together with interest; there was a degree of formality between them in public, which was in keeping with the atmosphere of their court, but he was in no doubt of their private happiness. Frederick was, however, still subject to moods, and his symptoms suggested what later ages would call manic depression – 'By fits and starts he is merry, but for the most part cogitative, or, as they here call it, melancholic,' Wotton wrote. The domestic differences which had caused Schomberg so much trouble appeared to have been settled, but the question of his late wife's replacement remained, and Elizabeth was anxious that her father should know her wishes on the subject. She wanted someone 'of no lesser quality than the former' and of no greater age, 'because otherwise she will be unfit to accompany her in her disports abroad'.

The eventual choice did not entirely fit that description, but it was one which Elizabeth entirely approved. Her old guardian's wife, the widowed Lady Harington, was given the appointment. 'The Lady Harington sets out on Tuesday or Wednesday towards Heidelberg, by the way of Flanders and Brabant,' wrote the indefatigable correspondent Mr Chamberlain to a friend on 23 November 1616. He added the titbit that there had been 'much ado to furnish her with £5,000 which the King bestows upon her'. Her daughter, Lady Bedford, expressed concern at her mother's undertaking so cruel a journey in the depths of winter, at her age, but knew that her love for the Princess Elizabeth was stronger than her fears. At all events, the elderly lady arrived safely, and was given a warm welcome by her former charge.

The following year saw the birth of Elizabeth's second child. Frederick hastened home from a protracted visit to the Upper Palatinate and his mother Louisa Juliana left the seclusion of her dower house to be present for the event. On 24 December the electress gave birth to her second son. Like Frederick Henry he was very dark in colouring, but unlike his brother he was a delicate baby, and there were fears about his health. It may have been his early fragility which aroused Elizabeth's strongest maternal feelings; it may have been some resemblance to her dead brother. At all events it was this child, and not the heir, or any of the eleven others who were to follow, who was to be her declared favourite during the coming years, even, as she later wrote unabashedly, while he was 'but a second son'.

The Queen of England and the Prince of Wales agreed to stand sponsor to the new baby, and the Electress Louisa Juliana and the Duke of Zweibrücken acted as their proxies at the christening ceremony. He was named Charles Louis, after the brothers of both his parents, and in London the customary bonfires were lit in celebration of his arrival.

Elizabeth lost none of her feelings for the country in which she had been brought up; though she had adapted happily and well to Heidelberg life, she longed to visit England again and see her family. 'The Lady Elizabeth, we hear, makes great means to come over hither, after she is fully recovered of her childbirth,' wrote Mr

Chamberlain, on 10 January 1618. She was, he went on, 'so bent to it that she will hardly be stayed'. He added somewhat sourly : 'I see not to what purpose it is, nor what good can come by it to either side; for unless here were a more plentiful world, she will not find that contentment she hath done heretofore, and expects.' Certainly Elizabeth's last memories of England were of a land of luxury and festivity, coloured by all the happiness of her wedding celebrations, but it was natural that she should have wanted to revisit her former home and see her parents and only brother again. The project had, however, to be abandoned for the time being when it became evident, in the spring of 1618, that the young electress was once more pregnant. As it turned out, she was never to see any of her immediate family again.

Queen Anne died of dropsy on 2 March 1619, at the age of forty-five, and Elizabeth grieved for her. Since her Scottish babyhood she had never been particularly close to her mother, and Anne had undoubtedly tried to discourage her marriage to Frederick, but Elizabeth was upset by the news of her death. 'It is so great an affliction to me that I have not the words to express it,' she wrote to King James. 'I pray God to console your Majesty, and for myself I am certain that I shall regret this death all my life.'

Despite Elizabeth's disappointment over the hoped-for visit to England, she had much to console her at Heidelberg. In the early hours of 27 November 1618, her third child was born; it was a girl. She was named Elizabeth. In looks she took after her father and brothers, dark-haired and brown-eyed, unlike her radiantly fair mother. Charles Louis was still the favourite, but all three children had to share their mother's affections with the growing menagerie of dogs and monkeys who barked and squealed around her apartments and romped on her bed in the mornings. Old Lady Harington wrote that the electress esteemed her pets as jewels, and another lady of honour, Mistress Apsley, informed Sir Dudley Carleton that young Frederick Henry was 'so fond of them as he says he desires nothing but such a monkey of his own'. She added : 'They do make very good sport, and her highness very merry; you could have sent nothing would a been more pleasing'. Elizabeth Apsley's own nickname was now 'Chief governor to all the monkeys and dogs'.

The married happiness of Elizabeth and Frederick continued to grow throughout these tranquil early years at Heidelberg. One observer wrote that Elizabeth was 'so dearly loving and beloved of the prince her husband that it is a joy to all that see them'. In their diplomatic marriage alliance Frederick and Elizabeth had found great personal happiness, and their enjoyment of their domestic life together was demonstrated by their pleasure in improving their castle and grounds. In 1614 Monsieur Solomon de Caus had been put in charge of extensive alterations to the gardens, and trees, plants, grottoes and alleyways had been laid out for Elizabeth's delight. The entrance to the 'English garden', said by local lore to have been built in a single night for the young electress, bore the inscription, 'Frederick v to his beloved wife Elizabeth, 1615'. During the years of their residence at Heidelberg the young couple carried out extensive building work on their castle, incorporating a new ballroom in the old round tower and constructing an entire new wing adjacent to the main building. A life-size statue of Frederick, wearing the Garter, was put up in Elizabeth's garden. Whatever nostalgic longings the Electress Palatine might sometimes feel for England, there could be no doubt that she had settled down contentedly to married life in Heidelberg.

By 1618, however, her peaceful Palatinate years were coming to an end. The political events in Bohemia which were about to raise Elizabeth and Frederick to a royal throne were in the end to destroy the peace and happiness of their life together.

The Upper Palatinate bordered on the kingdom of Bohemia, where the Emperor Matthias ruled as king. The throne of Bohemia, like that of the empire, was elective, but the House of Habsburg had come to look on it as their possession. However, though it remained in imperial Catholic hands, the kingdom had become a hotbed of Protestants. With this in mind, the ageing and childless Emperor Matthias made an unusual arrangement. To ensure that the kingdoms of Bohemia and Hungary should pass to a trusted Catholic kinsman on his death, he chose – with general Habsburg consent – to give the nominal rule of Bohemia and Hungary to his cousin the Archduke Ferdinand of Styria, in whose favour he would abdicate. Ferdinand was in his late thirties, a man of little personal distinction but impeccable in his Habsburg loyalties and Catholic faith. Although it was agreed that Matthias should continue as effective ruler during his lifetime, Ferdinand was elected King of Bohemia and crowned in Prague in July 1617.

Almost immediately he began to make his presence felt in harsh measures towards the Protestants in his new kingdom. As his Catholic subjects were, though powerful, in the minority, his actions provoked widespread resentment. Since the Protestants in Bohemia had received official liberty of conscience from Matthias in 1612, and had a cherished Letter of Majesty to confirm it, Ferdinand was in contravention of his coronation oaths, and the discontented Bohemians appealed to the elderly emperor. He did nothing to help them but indicated that Ferdinand had his absolute support. Outraged, the leaders of the Protestant dissenters, led by Count Thurn, decided on violent action. They made their intentions plain in the celebrated 'Defenestration of Prague', when they entered the old Hradschin Palace and, after an altercation, bodily flung the two chief supporters of the king and emperor, Martinitz and Slavata, out of the windows, rapidly followed by the secretary of the council, Fabricius. Miraculously all three survived the fall, but Count Thurn and his followers had made their belligerent point. Open revolt followed, and the rebellious Protestants raised an army under the command of Count Thurn.

A settlement was sought. It was suggested that two Protestants, the Elector Palatine and the Elector of Saxony, should act as mediators between the emperor and his rebel subjects. Neither side was prepared to compromise, however, and no agreement could be reached.

Young Frederick was deeply concerned. He turned to his father-in-law for advice and assistance; cautious and pacific as ever, James refused to become involved. His response was that he had only a defensive alliance with the German Protestant princes, and he told Frederick that he had no money for a religious war, although he let it be known that he had expended a large sum on a peace mission to the emperor. The only faintly hopeful note in his answer was an agreement to renew his alliance with the Union for a further period of four years.

In March 1619, there was a new development in Bohemia's troubled affairs when the Emperor Matthias died. The Elector Pala-tine summoned his fellow electors to a meeting at Frankfurt, as was his duty, to elect the new emperor. He himself did not attend, how-ever. Instead he sent deputies, with strict instructions not to cast his vote in favour of Ferdinand of Styria. 'It looks as though Ferdinand, instead of acquiring a crown at Frankfurt, may well lose two,' Frederick wrote to Elizabeth, adding with grim humour, 'He is a very fortunate prince, to have the pleasure of being hated by the entire world.' In the next sentence his letter took a pleasanter turn as he assured his 'dear heart', 'I wish I were with you, and I long for that happiness : in the meantime I ask you to love me always.'

On 18 August the fateful imperial election took place. The representative of the Elector Palatine cast his vote for Maximilian of Bavaria, Frederick's kinsman and the only Catholic candidate whom he supported. The Archbishop of Maine brought it to his attention, however, that the Duke of Bavaria had declined to stand, and had stated that all votes for him were to pass to the Archduke Ferdinand. There was nothing the Palatine deputy could do but vote again – for Ferdinand.

Ferdinand was duly proclaimed emperor. Elizabeth gave her opinion in round terms: 'They have chosen here a blind Emperor, for he hath but one eye, and that not very good. I am afraid he will be lousy, for he hath not money to buy himself clothes.' Mock the new emperor as she might, her own destiny was irrevocably bound up with his. Whilst he was being elected emperor at Frankfurt, Ferdinand of Styria was being replaced as king in Prague. He was declared deposed, and by an overwhelming majority the Bohemians chose as their new ruler the ardent young Protestant prince, head of

66

the Union, whose upper country bordered their own and whose father-in-law was the powerful King of England. As the cannon roared and bells pealed in Bohemia, the twenty-three-year-old Elizabeth Stuart, Electress Palatine, learned that she and her hushand had been offered a throne. She was about to become a queen.

CHAPTER FIVE
The Queen

The question now was whether or not Frederick should accept the honour. Tempting as the prospect of the Bohemian throne might be, both for his own advancement and for the good of Christendom, so glorious and hazardous a step could not be taken unadvisedly. Elizabeth did what she could to help her husband at this critical juncture in their lives.

'My Lord,' she wrote urgently to her father's influential favourite, the Marquis of Buckingham. 'This worthy bearer will inform you of a business that concerns his master very much: the Bohemians being desirous to choose him for their King, which he will not resolve of till he knows his Majesty's opinion in it.' Persuasively, she went on: 'The King hath now a good occasion to manifest to the world the love he hath ever professed to the Prince here. I earnestly entreat you to use your best means in persuading his Majesty to show himself now, in his helping of the Prince here, a true loving father to us both.'

Her 'true loving father' had, however, the interests of another, and still more important, child to consider at the same time. Negotiations were under way for the marriage of the nineteen-year-old Prince of Wales with the Infanta of Spain. However winningly Elizabeth might word her appeals to James's paternal affections, the circumspect King of England had no intention of alienating the Habsburgs by declaring his support for the Bohemian rebels in their opposition to the emperor. James I had married his daughter to the Elector Frederick not as proof of his total identification with the cause of the Union but as one part of a larger policy of forging links with both the Protestant and Habsburg powers.

It was an agonizing decision which now faced Frederick; the fate of nations literally depended upon his choice. As King of Bohemia he would have a second electoral vote to add to his own; he would rule a valuable kingdom, rich in both agriculture and trade; his territories would stretch from the Rhine to the Oder. But to accept would be tantamount to offering an open challenge to the hostile Catholic faction.

In his dilemma the young elector received a variety of conflicting counsels. For his devoted chancellor, Christian of Anhalt, the offer of the Bohemian crown was the longed-for outcome of months of political intriguing. The Archbishop of Canterbury, to whom Elizabeth had applied for advice, urged him to accept the glorious opportunity which God had sent. His mentor the Duke de Bouillon was likewise in favour, as were his respected uncle the Prince of Orange and his own chaplain, Scultetus, on whom he relied greatly. 'God forbid he should refuse it!' was the emphatic opinion of the English ambassador in Paris. From others, however, Frederick received very different advice. His own council voted against his acceptance, and his mother Louisa Juliana spoke out forthrightly, telling him not to endanger the interests of the Palatinate by involving himself in the troubled affairs of Bohemia. His kinsman Maximilian of Bavaria, head of the Catholic League which had since 1609 been in a state of cold war against the Protestant Union, forcefully warned him of the dangers of accepting: since Spain and all the Habsburgs were firmly ranged behind Ferdinand of Styria, for Frederick to replace him would be an act of deliberate defiance. To accept would be to rebel against the emperor and anger his powerful enemies; to refuse would be to turn down a unique opportunity to advance both the Protestant faith and himself. What was he to do?

Elizabeth has traditionally been accused of using every means in her power to persuade Frederick to accept the hazardous challenge.

In fact she left the final decision entirely to him. Her own attitude was one of restrained enthusiasm; she wrote to tell her beloved husband that he had her full support in whatever course he might decide to take. It was apparent that she hoped he would accept; she betrayed her feelings in her request for King James's support for Frederick and her assurances that she would willingly face whatever consequences might result from his decision. But such cautious encouragement could not be said to amount to undue pressure.

In the last resort it was Frederick's devout conscience which decided the matter. 'It is a divine call which I ought not to refuse,' he wrote to the Duke de Bouillon. His mind was made up. On 18 September he agreed to meet a contingent of Bohemian deputies on the frontier between his Upper country and theirs; if the terms they offered were satisfactory, he would agree to be proclaimed their king.

During this fateful autumn Elizabeth was once again in a state of advanced pregnancy. She would not, however, allow her condition to prevent her from sharing in her husband's triumphal journey to his new kingdom. She made her feelings clear to James I's envoy Lord Doncaster, who was visiting Heidelberg. Frederick told Doncaster that he was not sure whether Elizabeth should remain in the Palatinate, go to England for a time, or travel to Bohemia by his side; Doncaster was able to assure the elector that 'her own vehement inclination and almost inexorableness to the contrary, drew her to accompany him'. Elizabeth Stuart had never lacked spirit, and she was not the woman to miss such an adventure as this. 'To express her love to him, and her desire to participate in all his fortunes', she had set her heart on joining Frederick on the great journey.

It was arranged that the two younger children should stay behind in Heidelberg under the solicitous eye of their grandmother, while the eldest, six-year-old Frederick Henry, was to make the journey to Prague with his parents. On the morning of 27 September the royal party set out. An eye-witness named John Harrison printed a brief account of their departure. 'About 8 of the clock, these princely personages,' he wrote, 'with their train, in their caroches and some on horses and wagons, without any vain pomp or ostentation, but rather tears in their eyes lifted up to heaven, quietly departed.' He declared sentimentally, 'no heart but would have been ravished to have seen the sweet demeanour of that great lady' who, in an echo of John Donne's wedding-poem, he described as being 'like another Queen Elizabeth revived also again in her, the only Phoenix of the world'. The dangers of the undertaking on which Elizabeth was setting out were very much to the forefront of Harrison's thoughts. 'It is the manner of the Moors', he informed his readers, 'in their most deadly battles, to make choice of one of their chiefest and fairest virgins to go before them into the field.' That Elizabeth, heavily pregnant with her fourth child, should have inspired such a simile was a tribute to the continuing charm of her looks and manner. Harrison's intention was not merely to eulogize King James's daughter and son-in-law, but to rouse the spirits of patriotic Englishmen to support them in the crusade on which they were embarking. 'And to this service of Almighty God against the enemies of his church, this noble and religious young prince hath wholly devoted himself,' he wrote, and added that Frederick had gone so far as to give away his pack of hounds 'and other things pertaining to his pleasure', so that pastimes should not distract him from his holy mission. 'And shall we suffer our sweet princess, our royal infanta, the only daughter of our sovereign lord and king, to go before us into the field, and not follow after her!' he demanded rhetorically. To heighten the drama of Elizabeth's situation, Harrison depicted her as setting out with tears trickling poetically down her cheeks.

Whether or not she shed tears on leaving her first married home for the strange and danger-filled land of Bohemia, Elizabeth had plenty to interest and distract her on the journey. After a short visit to the Margrave of Ansbach, she and Frederick reached the major city of Amberg, in the Upper Palatinate, on 4 October. There Frederick had to face an imperial envoy, sent to represent to him the significance of his disobedience to the Emperor Ferdinand and to beg him to reconsider his decision. The new King of Bohemia was not to be swayed, however, and soon he and his wife and their 153 baggage waggons were once more rumbling along the dusty roads towards the Bohemian frontier, accompanied now by a thousand troops.

In the border town of Waldsassen Elizabeth gave her first audience as queen to a contingent of Bohemian deputies. Baron Rupa, one of the Protestant leaders responsible for the Defenestration of Prague, addressed her in French. He thanked her for her help in persuading Frederick to accept their crown, and – with tragic irony – wished her a long reign. Elizabeth replied to his speech with regal charm. 'Sir, what I have done for the honour of God and the good of our religion has been done whole-heartedly,' she told him. 'You may be assured that in future my love and affection shall not be found wanting.' A church service and a banquet followed, and on the following day Elizabeth and her husband crossed for the first time into their new country.

For once Elizabeth broke her lifelong custom of never travelling on a Sunday; speed was important on this journey. On 21 October 1619, the new king and queen ceremonially entered Prague. Proceedings began half a mile outside the city, at the royal lodge of the Star Park. There the grand chamberlain, Baron Burka, and the burgesses of Prague came to greet Frederick and attend him into the city. With Frederick riding on a great horse and Elizabeth travelling in a beautifully decorated coach, they made their way into their new capital. Outside the walls they had a bizarre encounter with a four hundred-strong group of Hussite peasants, armed with scythes, flails, hatchets and targets; they rattled their homely weapons in greeting, and made such a 'tintamarre' of rustic noise that Frederick and Elizabeth could not help laughing, just as six years earlier they had been unable to stop themselves giggling at their own solemn marriage service. Their amusement died away when they saw the vast throngs of people waiting in the city to see them pass. Frederick was perturbed by the size of the crowds, and gave orders that no cannon salutes were to be fired in such a mass of humanity, in case anyone should be injured. It seemed that the new king was received with genuine joy. The Habsburg oppressor had gone, and in his place the Bohemians had this slight, handsome young man, who was prepared to risk danger to be their ruler, and with him his fair and fecund wife. It was a day of heartfelt rejoicing in Prague. 'We arrived here being received with a great show of love of all sorts of people,' Elizabeth was able to inform her father's favourite, Buckingham, with evident satisfaction.

At about five o'clock in the afternoon the royal couple reached their new residence, the Hradschin Palace. That night Elizabeth insisted on sharing her husband's lodgings. She was Queen of Bohemia now, but she was also a twenty-three-year-old girl in a strange country.

On 25 October she sat in a high private gallery in the Cathedral of St Vitus, and watched her husband receive his crown. It was the greatest moment of Frederick's life. The coronation ceremony was very long, and there had been difficulties over the question of whether or not he should be anointed; the rite had unfortunate overtones of Catholicism, and while the Lutherans had kept the practice, the Calvinists, of whom the Elector Palatine was one, had rejected it. It was eventually agreed that Frederick should receive the holy oil, but his chaplain Scultetus refused to be a party to such a service and stayed away. The music was sublime however, and the people demonstrated their excessive joy at the coronation of their chosen king.

Three days later Elizabeth's own crowning took place. It was shorter than Frederick's, but very gorgeous. In the chapel of St Wenceslas she was dressed in her royal robes, and then she was led into the church, where she walked solemnly to the altar behind the clergymen and Bohemian officials. As she sat in state on the throne, prayers were said for her long and peaceful reign. Frederick took part in the ceremony; it fell to him to address the venerable priest in Latin with the words, 'Oh reverend father, we request that thou wilt deign to bless this our consort, joined to us by God, and decorate her with the crown royal, to the praise and glory of our Saviour Jesus Christ.'

The bells of Prague pealed in rejoicing, the crowds cheered and shouted and cannon were shot off as Elizabeth was ceremonially led back to the palace, where a splendid banquet was laid out. Unlike Frederick, the young queen did not scatter money among her subjects; instead, she gave orders that bread and wine were to be distributed. 'Their majesties', ran a contemporary newsletter, 'conduct themselves altogether with such amiable grace, that they gain and attract the hearts of all, so that they know not how to praise them enough.' The reign of the Winter King and Queen of Bohemia had begun well.

A small incident which took place on the feast day of St Elizabeth temporarily clouded Elizabeth's popularity among her female subjects; it was soon passed over, but it was received at the time as a slight to her new countrywomen. A group of citizens' wives were permitted to come to the palace and enter the queen's presence with a gift of loaves of bread baked in the shape of flowers – a pretty memorial to an earlier Queen Elizabeth of Hungary, the saint whose charitable works wrought a miracle. Found by her stern husband to be carrying an apronful of objects, and asked what they were, she lied and said 'Flowers', to conceal the fact that she was taking bread to the poor. When she was made to reveal the contents of her apron her words came true, and the loaves were transformed into colourful blossoms. Perhaps Elizabeth Stuart had never heard the touching story; perhaps she was merely unused to being given presents consisting of bread. At all events, she received the women's gift with less than her usual grace, and the rumour quickly spread throughout Prague that the sophisticated new queen had allowed her servants to make mock of the simple offering.

Fortunately, Elizabeth had the means to redeem herself in her subjects' eyes very shortly after that incident. A subsequent, more welcome, present received at the palace was a gorgeous jewel-studded cradle for the new baby about to be born, and on 7 December 1619, Elizabeth was delivered of her third son. He was another fine healthy 'black babie', and the Bohemians were overjoyed. He was given the name of Rupert, in honour of a former Elector Palatine who had become King of Bohemia, and for a time many Bohemians hoped that this baby prince, born in their country, might be declared the heir to their throne. This was not Frederick's intention, however, and he lost no opportunity of demonstrating that little Frederick Henry, who had accompanied his parents from Heidelberg as the heir, was to inherit all his domains. For Rupert of the Rhine, born amid the splendours of his parents' year of majesty, and rocked in a jewelled cradle, a very different life lay ahead.

'The King hath bidden Bethlen Gabor, the Prince of Transylvania, to christen this little boy,' Elizabeth wrote gaily to her dear friend Lady Bedford, the Haringtons' daughter. She added, 'Many put it out that he is half a Turk. But I assure you it is not so.' At the christening ceremony, which took place on Sunday, 31 March in the cathedral of St Vitus, the exotic Transylvanian godfather sent the baby boy a present of a spirited Turkish stallion, bearing a lavishly ornamented saddle and bridle. Sumptuous celebrations followed Prince Rupert's baptism.

In April the Estates of Bohemia met, and gave their official recognition to Frederick Henry as crown prince. The proclamation was greeted not only by a cannon salute but by three loud claps of thunder – a good omen, it was said at the time, though in retrospect it must have appeared otherwise.

It was ironic that even while the Bohemians were providing for the future of Frederick and Elizabeth's ruling dynasty in naming Frederick Henry as their crown prince, the Emperor Ferdinand was priming the war-machine which was shortly to drive them and their children from Bohemia altogether. In March a meeting took place at Mühlhausen, in which Frederick's action in accepting the Bohemian crown was considered. His argument, that he had taken the crown merely from Ferdinand the Austrian archduke, and not from Ferdinand the Holy Roman Emperor, was found to be invalid. Frederick had broken his allegiance and disrupted the imperial peace; he had thereby rendered himself liable for the severest retribution. Late in April the emperor issued an ultimatum. Frederick was given one month in which to quit Bohemia. Frederick refused. From then on he was under the imperial ban; it had become the duty of every loyal subject of the empire, including his own people in the Palatinate, to

oppose him by force. As a usurper, he must be cast out of the territories which he had wrongfully possessed. War had ceased to be a
threat, and become a certainty.

During the months which followed Frederick did what he could
to rally support, both at home and abroad. He visited the outposts of
his territories in person, and sent out appeals for help to the Protestant
powers. He received little encouragement. The German Protestant
princes, like the King of England, were anxious not to involve themselves in a war against the Habsburg powers. The King of France,
Louis XIII, declined to take sides in the matter. James I allowed a
small expeditionary force, commanded by Sir Horace Vere, to set out
for the Palatinate early in July, but he still refused to throw the might
of England behind his son-in-law's cause, which effectively discouraged others from doing so. 'His Majesty hath a purpose to join
with the French King in doing all good offices for the weal of
Christendom to pacify the present broils that are on foot in Germany,'
was the bland explanation from Whitehall.

Within Bohemia itself Frederick's position was not as strong as it
might have been. There had long been dissent between the different
Protestant factions, and Frederick's Calvinist beliefs had caused problems from the time of his coronation service onwards. And he had
inadvertently caused great offence to his new subjects in a matter very
close to their hearts. On the bridge over the Moldau there had long
stood a crucifix, flanked by carved wooden figures of the Virgin and
saints. Frederick's officious chaplain, Scultetus, affronted by the
presence of such idols in a Protestant capital, arranged for their
removal. The people of Prague were outraged. The figures were
regarded as national monuments, and that Frederick should have
countenanced such an act of disrespect was deeply resented by the
Bohemian people. When public feeling in the matter was made
known to him the young king hastily had the carvings restored, but
his reputation had suffered, and blame was even attached to Elizabeth, who, it was rumoured, had sworn never to cross the bridge
while the statues stood there.

In fact, Elizabeth had always had considerable regard for public opinion. On her wedding journey, and after, she had made largely successful efforts to win the good graces of her subjects in the Palatinate, and in her letters from Bohemia she frequently referred with satisfaction to the people's displays of love for Frederick and herself. She was not always lucky in her attempts to win the approval of the citizens of Prague, however. Her foreign dresses and fashionable style of hairdressing were regarded with suspicious curiosity, and some of her actions made her mistrusted. On one occasion a conscious attempt to win herself popularity misfired. At a public feast she was served with her food and drink by Bohemians instead of her usual servants. It was an unfortunate experiment. Wine was spilt on her expensive dress, the food was tipped off her plate before it reached her, and one of her monkeys terrified a waiting-man by leaping, gibbering excitedly, onto his shoulder and snatching sugar from him. The incident did nothing to endear the foreign queen to her new countrymen.

Yet among those who spoke her language, both literally and metaphorically, Elizabeth was able to inspire unshakeable loyalty and love. One friend who committed himself to her cause for life was the English diplomat Sir Thomas Roe. A former friend of Elizabeth's adored brother Henry, he was a worldly, much-travelled man of considerable wealth; when Elizabeth became Queen of Bohemia Roe had recently returned from the court of the Mogul Emperor of India, where he had been James I's ambassador. 'I see your journey hath not altered you in your true professing of your love to me,' Elizabeth wrote fondly. 'Honest fat Thom', as she called him, had taken up the cause of Frederick and the Bohemian Protestants, and had printed a pamphlet in their support. 'I thank you for the love you have written concerning the Bohemians, it is exceeding well done, I showed it to the King he likes it very well and commends him to you, he says you do so much for him as he knows not how to requite you,' Elizabeth told him. She added a postscript: 'Your old friend my monkey is in very good health here and commands all my women with his teeth.' The time was coming when Elizabeth would have need of friends such as Thomas Roe.

Another ardent admirer of the beautiful Winter Queen expressed his feelings in verse during the summer of 1620. It was Sir Henry Wotton, another of King James's ambassadors, who wrote the celebrated poem:

> You meaner beauties of the night
> That poorly satisfy our eyes
> More by your number than your light,
> You common people of the skies,
> What are you when the moon shall rise?
>
> You curious chanters of the wood
> That warble forth Dame Nature's lays,
> Thinking your passions understood
> By your weak accents; what's your praise
> When Philomel her voice shall raise?
>
> You violets that first appear
> By your pure purple mantles known,
> Like the proud virgins of the year
> As if the spring were all your own;
> What are you when the rose is blown?
>
> So, when my mistress shall be seen
> In form and beauty of her mind,
> By virtue first, then choice, a Queen,
> Tell me if she were not designed
> Th' eclipse and glory of her kind.

Elizabeth Stuart had been cast in the role of a heroine, not only by the diplomats and courtiers who knew her personally but by the common people of England. From her earliest years the lively, fair-haired princess had been a popular figure; her marriage had captured the public imagination, and her elevation to the role of queen of a faraway country and wife of a Protestant champion had set the seal on loyal Englishmen's enthusiasm for her. Sir Thomas Roe wrote to tell her so – 'I may assure your Majesty a joyful truth, I never shall see any so beloved here that dwells not here, nor any cause so affected as yours.' It was not the people of England, but her 'own true loving father', who was to fail Elizabeth when she was in need.

Though life at the Hradschin Palace proceeded with apparent calm during the summer of 1620, the storm was about to break. Spain and Bavaria – Maximilian of Bavaria being the head of the Catholic League – had been bound from the outset to aid their kinsman and emperor, Ferdinand of Styria; the Elector Frederick's acceptance of the deposed Ferdinand's crown had been an open invitation to war, and now, with the weak Union of Protestant Princes and the exotic Bethlen Gabor of Transylvania as his only allies, he had to face the consequences. The Queen of Bohemia's new English secretary, Sir Francis Nethersole, wrote of the 'dangerous and almost desperate state of affairs of this kingdom'. And from Heidelberg, late in August, James I received a letter containing terrible news. 'It is now too late to doubt whether Spinola's great army is designed against the Palatinate,' wrote a terrified Electress Louisa Juliana. 'It is already at our gates.' Of the four powerful armies under the emperor's control, the Spanish had been the first to march, under their able commander the Genoese-born Ambrogio Spinola. On 18 August Spinola's troops crossed the border and entered the Lower Palatinate from the Spanish Netherlands, heading for Heidelberg. Desperately, the electress appealed to the King of England's paternal feelings. 'Your Majesty will know also in what distress the Queen your daughter is, and that she is about to be completely surrounded by enemies. The condition in which I left her makes me doubly pity her.' At this moment of crisis Elizabeth was once again pregnant. Louisa Juliana's immediate concern was for the two small children left in her care; with Prince Charles Louis and the two-year-old Princess Elizabeth she fled from Heidelberg to safety.

The young Queen of Bohemia knew better than to try appealing solely to her father, against whose better judgement she and her husband had mounted their disputed throne. She sent an imploring letter to her affectionate younger brother :

My only dear brother, I am sure you have heard before this that

Spinola hath taken some towns in the Lower Palatinate, which makes me trouble you with these lines, to beseech you earnestly to move his Majesty that now he would assist us; for he may easily see how little his embassages are regarded. Dear brother, be most earnest with him, for to speak freely to you, his slackness to assist us doth make the Princes of the Union slack too, who do nothing with their army; the King hath ever said that he would not suffer the Palatinate to be taken; it was never in hazard but now, and I beseech you again, dear brother, to solicit as much as you can, for her that loves you more than all the world.

Prince Charles sent her £2,000 of his own money, but even he was powerless to alter King James's declared policy of meditation into one of armed intervention.

As the second, Bavarian, army began to march on Bohemia, the exodus from the threatened city of Prague began. Crown Prince Frederick Henry was sent away to safety, but Elizabeth herself, with characteristic courage, refused to leave. Sir Francis Nethersole reported in a despatch dated 5 September that she was 'irremovably resolved to abide still in this town'. She had made up her mind, he wrote, 'out of her rare and admirable love to the king her husband', on the grounds that the Bohemians might be disheartened if she were to abandon the country while the king was with the army; she believed her departure 'might be the occasion of much danger'. Nethersole assured King James that he had done all he could to persuade her to change her mind, 'but her Majesty hath at last silenced me'. Elizabeth's resolve was all the more admirable in view of her conviction that the dreaded Spinola would not hesitate to 'seize upon her person', since he had shown no scruples about invading the Palatinate. While King James of England relied on 'embassages' instead of force of arms to defend his daughter's rights, her enemies need not fear to do as they chose with her.

'God grant that it will not be necessary for you to leave Prague!' Frederick wrote to Elizabeth on 1 November. He had taken every precaution for his adored wife's safety before departing to join his army; he had disarmed all Catholics who refused the oath of allegiance; he had arranged for two companies of troops to stay behind to defend the city; he had made provision for the functions of civil government to be carried out as before, and he had left his own bodyguard to protect the queen. There was, however, little he could do to guard her against depression. His letters home were full of injunctions to her to keep her spirits up; 'I beg you not to be melancholy, and assure you that you will ever be perfectly loved by me,' he wrote in early October. He went on, 'I hope that God will preserve us for many more years together; but for the love of God have a care for your health, if not out of regard for yourself, at least for love of me, of our dear children, and of the dear little one; and do not give way to melancholy.' He ended with a postscript concerning the two ambassadors from King James, Conway and Weston, who had arrived in Prague after a series of fruitless visits to the Catholic courts of Europe; he bade Elizabeth tell them 'that there is no one who desires peace more than me, as long as it be honourable to their master and me; but to quit the kingdom can be so to neither'. Frederick paid a fleeting visit to Prague to meet these ambassadors, and left them convinced that whatever concessions he might make, he would never be prevailed upon to give up the Bohemian crown.

In a despatch written from the Hradschin Palace, Sir Francis Nethersole reported, 'We can in this town hear the cannon play day and night, which were enough to fright another Queen. Her Majesty is nothing troubled therewith.' Despite Elizabeth's courage and resolve, Frederick began to feel, uneasily, that she should prepare for sudden departure from her capital; writing in French, as usual, he commented,

God grant that it may not be necessary! Anyway, it can do no harm to be prepared; for likewise, if necessity requires it, all will take place in great confusion ... Tell me honestly if you yourself do not think it would be better for you to leave Prague in good order, than to wait until the enemy approach nearer and let it turn into something more resembling a flight.

The imperial forces, under the command of the able cavalry general Count Tilly, were indeed coming closer to Prague, but at the moment of their greatest danger the inhabitants of the Hradschin Palace enjoyed a brief, delusory sense of security. On 7 November, Frederick, with 'a countenance of glee', announced that the enemy was within eight miles of the city, but that his own army 'was betwixt them and it'. That night, reported Conway, 'we slept securely, as free from doubt, as we supposed ourselves quit from danger'. On the following day, 'while we were at our cups, the enemy was upon a march towards us'. News was brought that the Bohemian cavalry, which had spent the night in the Star Park, former scene of so many happy hunting-parties, 'upon the outflanks of the army did skirmish'. Still Frederick seemed confident, and the general opinion was that neither army was eager for battle. After dinner the young king announced his intention of going to inspect his troops on horseback. 'But before the king could get out of the gate', Conway reported laconically, 'the news came of the loss of the Bohemian cannon, and the disorder of all the squadrons, both of horse and foot.' The Battle of the White Mountain was well advanced, and Frederick's army was being utterly routed. Those who had jeered that Frederick and Elizabeth would prove a 'Winter King and Queen of Snow' had been proved right.

There was no more debating. The moment had come for Elizabeth to leave and, as Frederick had feared, her departure took the form of a flight. The enemy was in pursuit, and the citizens of Prague were milling about the streets in a state of panic. Christian of Anhalt, Frederick's supreme general, was one of the terrified fugitives from the battle begging for admission to the palace.

Elizabeth's courage did not fail her; with her hastily packed personal possessions she stepped into her carriage and was soon jolting past the hysterical crowds. She was too distracted to think of everything, however, and one precious item was nearly left behind in the confusion. As the last of the royal cavalcade was departing, Baron Christopher Dohna rushed up, breathless and panting, wrenched open the boot of the coach and tipped something in. Only when the muffled bundle began to howl furiously did the startled occupants of the coach realize that the infant Prince Rupert had almost been left to the invaders. Many a mother's first thought in such a crisis would have been for her baby; Elizabeth Stuart's detachment where children were concerned was one of the less sympathetic aspects of her coolly courageous personality.

The Queen of Bohemia was carried swiftly away from her palace, across the bridge whose statues had caused such disputes. 'Now art thou carried whither thou wouldst not go,' jeered a Catholic writer of the time. Considerable blame was unfairly attached to her as having been the cause of Frederick's absence from his army at the moment when his presence at its head was most needed. He had slipped away to see his wife and thereby missed the battle. Even Sir Francis Nethersole, who considered the king's absence from the fighting to have been providential, considering the danger to his person, felt obliged to point out that 'his presence would have had much power to make his men stand better'. Christian of Anhalt was also blamed by contemporary report for his 'unanswerable and unparalleled unworthiness' in leaving the field.

'I hope still well, in spite of all,' Elizabeth had written bravely, a few weeks before; now, turned out of her home, heavily pregnant, with her world in total disorder, her gallant spirit remained indomitable. According to the ambassadors Conway and Weston, Frederick maintained a clearness of judgement, constancy and assurance throughout the crisis which they much admired, considering that his honour, fortune and all worldly happiness were at stake, but 'his incomparable lady, who truly saw the state she was in, did not let fall herself below the dignity of a queen, and kept the freedom of her countenance and discourse, with such an unchangeable temper, as at once did raise in all capable men this one thought – that her mind could not be brought under fortune.' It was a frightening journey on which she embarked; heading for the Silesian border the Winter King and Queen travelled through heavy snow, lacking many of their most precious belongings, and attended by a scared and unreliable entourage. At one stage Elizabeth, despite her condition, was obliged to ride pillion for forty miles behind a young Englishman named Ralph Hopton; as a Cavalier general, Hopton was to perform still greater services for her brother Charles I some twenty years later.

Finding shelter for the dispossessed queen did not prove easy. Halting at Breslau, in Silesia, where Frederick had been rapturously welcomed as king only a year before, the couple tried to make plans. It was decided that they should appeal to Frederick's brother-in-law, the Elector of Brandenburg. George William of Brandenburg proved an unwelcoming host, terrified of antagonizing the conquering emperor. He made every possible excuse, representing to Elizabeth the patent unsuitability of his royal residences for a distressed queen about to give birth, but by now Elizabeth had little choice. Leaving Frederick to raise levies in loyal Silesia and Moravia, she travelled on with a small escort and arrived safely at the castle of Custrin, about fifty miles outside Berlin. There, amid bitter snow and ice, she waited for her confinement. Despite the discomforts of her situation there was one consolation: at least the Winter King's fifth child would not be born by the wayside.

On 29 November she wrote to her beloved aunt the Duchess de la Trémoille, and told her, 'I comfort myself with one thought, that the war is not over yet; and I hope that God has only done this to test us, but I do not doubt that in the end he will give us the best of it, for the love of his church.' She added on an uncharacteristic note of pathos, 'I am spending the winter in this country, where I feel I am in exile.' She was more her usual self in the postscript to her accompanying letter to the countess's son; she told him gaily he would 'laugh heartily about the fine journey we have had'. The ability to joke about her own misfortunes was one of Elizabeth Stuart's most heroic qualities.

When the imperial forces marched into Prague, Te Deums were sung in churches of all denominations. Moravia, on the point of being invaded, made peace with the emperor. Silesia, with courteous words and a large bribe, implored Frederick to take himself to a place of safety. On 13 December, quoting an appropriate biblical reference to David and Absalom, Frederick set off with tears in his eyes to join his wife at Custrin.

In London rumours spread rapidly that Queen Elizabeth was dead in childbed, having given birth to a premature, stillborn baby. On 6 January 1621 she proved them wrong: in an easy labour lasting little more than an hour she produced another healthy, dark-faced son. He was given the name of Maurice, in honour of his paternal great-uncle, the Prince of Orange; the compliment was to be amply repaid in the months and years that followed his beleaguered birth.

Writing to tell the King of England of the birth of his latest grand-child, Frederick begged for assistance for his family. James's response to their miserable plight was, characteristically, more 'embassages'. Sir Edward Villiers, brother of the gorgeous Marquis of Bucking-ham, was despatched to the dethroned king and queen with a promise of £20,000 as a New Year's gift. The English were hot to help the beloved Lady Elizabeth and her husband; James announced to Parlia-ment that if peaceful means were unavailing he was ready to spill his own and his son's blood in his daughter's cause. They were fine words, and they committed him to nothing.

When Villiers arrived at the chilly castle of Custrin he found the King of Bohemia subdued and ready to submit to his father-in-law's judgement. Frederick signed a document agreeing to renounce his claim to the Bohemian throne if his birthright in the Palatinate were restored to him; it proved a useless concession, since his enemies were already firmly in possession of both, the Spanish in the Lower Palatin-ate, Bavaria in the Upper, and the emperor intended that they should remain so.

Frederick's fortunes were at a low ebb in the early weeks of 1621. A year before he had been the elected king of one prosperous country and the hereditary ruler of another; now he had lost everything, and the future of his ever-increasing family looked bleak. He was not even permitted to suffer with dignity. It was part of his enemies' policy to make him look as foolish as possible, and a clever propaganda campaign of abusive mockery was under way against the hapless 'King of Snow'. One of the many caricatures which were circulated showed him perched on the Wheel of Fortune, while the verses below jeered,

> Formerly he had many folk and lands,
> Now he has an empty hand.
> Formerly he had a crown on his head,
> Now he has scarcely a whole shirt to wear.
> God help poor Frederick
> He will never recover.

Among the Winter King's plundered possessions was his precious Garter, and his enemies seized the opportunity to twit him with its loss; a garterless king, his stocking falling down like a schoolboy's, was shown in cartoons. Pictures of 'A Post Boy Looking for a Missing King' were circulated, and Elizabeth, who was generally blamed for having brought Frederick to this pass by forcing him to accept the Bohemian crown, was satirically depicted as a lioness with a brood of young.

The Elector of Brandenburg found his guests both expensive and embarrassing. The emperor sent him a mandate that he was 'not to harbour the King in his dominions, nor to suffer the Queen to stay in them longer than he could truly excuse it upon her Majesty's ability to go on', as it was reported. It was time for the fugitives to move on.

The suggestion that they might find an honourable refuge in England was swiftly vetoed by King James. He was still involved in complicated negotiations for a Spanish marriage for the Prince of Wales, and the last thing he wanted was to be seen harbouring the usurping King and Queen of Bohemia, quite apart from the expense of providing for their bevy of children and large entourage. There was no doubt that the English would have welcomed the return of their beloved Elizabeth, but that was in itself a reason why James did not want her to come: once in England she might have become the popular rallying-point for the growing forces of Puritan opposition. To scotch rumours that Sir Edward Villiers had been sent over for the express purpose of inviting her, James made his wishes painfully clear to his daughter and son-in-law. Hurt as she must have been, Elizabeth responded to the slight with great dignity. She gave out that it was her own wish that they should not go to England; Nethersole reported, 'the queen herself hath no inclination to it, and hath given Sir Edward Villiers commission to make her answers known to the King her father; who, I presume, will not send for her against her will.'

Another, more distant, relation proved hospitable, however. The bachelor Prince of Orange was soon to resume hostilities against the Spanish after a twelve-year truce, but he sent a warm invitation to the Winter King and Queen to go to The Hague. He would make a suitable town residence available to them, and in the summer Elizabeth would be welcome to make use of his palace at Breda, while Frederick was with his army. It seemed the ideal solution. The States-General were sympathetic to Frederick's cause, and The Hague would provide a peaceful home, within reach both of England and Germany. The Prince of Orange was gratifyingly pressing in his invitation. King James gave his thankful approval to the step, and the decision was made.

The Prince of Orange's little namesake was left in Berlin under the care of the Elector of Brandenburg's wife, and Elizabeth and Frederick embarked on their journey to The Hague. The route they took must have awakened memories of an earlier, happier, voyage, as one by one they passed the towns and villages which had welcomed Elizabeth as a young bride on her triumphal wedding-journey. At Rotterdam they were received by the English ambassador, Sir Dudley Carleton, and his wife; it was a happy reunion. A great throng of people turned out to see the exiles arrive, and at The Hague the crowds were said to have wept with sympathy for the beautiful and unfortunate queen who had come to live among them. Their host escorted them into the town in state, and they were lodged, as they had been on their wedding-progress, in his brother Henry's apartments.

By 9 April a more permanent residence had been found for them. Two large, elegant houses standing side by side, one empty, the

D

other the property of a political exile, and still lived in by his wife, were made over to the use of the King and Queen of Bohemia. The Wassanaer Hof, in which Madam van der Myle was allowed to keep a small set of apartments, was a fine old red-brick house, set in its own courtyard. Outside it was lavishly adorned with sloping roofs, gables, chimneys and dormer windows; inside it had been lovingly decorated and furnished by its previous owner. To ensure that it should be worthy of its royal inhabitants, the States made provision for further redecoration and furnishings. With its stone floors and wooden ceilings, its walls covered with silk and leather and its rich tapestries and pictures, it made a comfortable and attractive home, even for a queen accustomed to palaces.

When Elizabeth arrived at the Wassanaer Hof in the spring of 1621 the most colourful phase of her life was over. Henceforth she would live in the stately, peaceful surroundings of The Hague, among the prosperous and respectable Dutch. The exiled queen had done with wandering; for the next forty years this was to be her home.

CHAPTER SIX
The Distressed Lady

'I do not look for any good change of fortune for us if my father do no more than he hath done,' Elizabeth wrote to her old friend 'Honest fat Thom' Roe on 11 May 1621. Though she added with satisfaction, 'I have very good company here', and told him that she was too busy receiving guests to write to his wife for the time being, she had much to be despondent about. 'The Palatinate grows worse and worse,' she had written to another friend a few days before, and she warned her father plainly, 'The Palatinate is in danger of being utterly lost, if your Majesty give us not some aid.'

The news that came out of Bohemia in July was depressing for the former king and queen. Appalling reprisals were being taken against their adherents; torture and execution were the order of the day, and severed heads now adorned the great bridge across the river. It was rumoured that to show his contempt for the rights of the Bohemian Protestants, Ferdinand had ripped the seal off their all-important Letter of Majesty. Clearly the victorious emperor was in no mood to come to terms.

The exiled king's melancholia returned with such force that his wife was perturbed. The news that yet another 'embassage' from the King of England had yielded no results, and Lord Digby had failed to effect a renewal of the truce in the Palatinate despite his efforts in Vienna, brought on a severe bout of the depression which had dogged Frederick for so long. 'The King is much troubled at the news, more than ever I saw him,' Elizabeth confided to the Marquis of Buckingham on 8 July. She begged him to use his influence with King James, 'to get his majesty to send him so effectual comfortable answer that may a little ease his melancholy, for I confess it troubles me to see him so'. In August Frederick took steps to find his own remedy; he joined the army of the Prince of Orange, who was now at war with Spain, as a volunteer. In his distress nothing was worse than inactivity.

By the end of 1621 the beautiful exiled Queen of Bohemia had become something of a cult among gallant young men in England and Europe. It was reported that

> The Lieutenant of the Middle Temple played a game this Christmastide whereat his Majesty was highly displeased. He made choice of some three of the civillest and best-fashioned gentlemen of that house to sup with him, and being at supper, took a cup of wine in one hand and held his sword drawn in the other, and so began a health 'to the distressed Lady Elizabeth', and having drunk, kissed his sword and laying his hand upon it, took an oath to live and die in her service.

One young man who showed himself literally willing to die in Elizabeth's service was her twenty-two-year-old 'cousin of Brunswick', Prince Christian. A brother of the Duke of Brunswick-Wolfenbüttel, he loved the martial life, and he found in the cause of the beautiful Winter Queen an ideal opportunity to combine romance and soldiering. He conceived a desperate passion for her in the courtly-love tradition which had so delighted her godmother Elizabeth 1; he wore her glove in his hat, his banners bore the motto 'For God and for her', and he wrote to her that he was 'Your most humble, constant, faithful, affectionate and obedient slave, who loves you and will love you, infinitely and unceasingly, till death'. However nonsensical his emotional attachment, 'the mad Halberstadter', as he was nicknamed, had much to offer in military terms. During the autumn of 1621 he succeeded in raising a ten-thousand-strong army with which to march to the defence of his beloved lady's rights.

Another useful ally for Frederick, who was inspired by very different motives, was George Frederick, Margrave of Baden-Durlach. A deeply religious Calvinist and German patriot, his determination to combat the Spanish menace caused him to raise an army numbering eleven thousand with which to fight for the restoration of the Palatinate. A third source of military assistance for Frederick was provided by the unpredictable but intermittently brilliant Ernest, Count Mansfeld. By the spring of 1622 some forty thousand men could be called on by Frederick to fight in his cause.

Clean-shaven and in disguise, the Winter King once again took leave of his wife at The Hague at the end of March, 1622, and by early April he was buying little presents for her in Paris, on his way to join his forces in the Palatinate. He had left Elizabeth once again on the point of giving birth, but as he reminded her in a letter, she generally had an easy time of it : 'It is a great mercy that God grants you.' Two weeks after his departure, in the early morning of 8 April, his sixth child was born. This time it was a girl. As was usual with the children of Frederick and Elizabeth, political tact dictated their choice of names; this second daughter was given the Christian names Louise Hollandine, in combined compliment to her grandmother and her parents' host-country, the States of Holland. A grand christening took place on 16 April. The Dutch States were among the godparents; their practical gift to the new baby was a life pension of two hundred pounds. The devoted Christian of Brunswick was also a generous godfather; with typical outlandish charm he sent the little girl his latest ransom from a prisoner-of-war.

While Elizabeth was busy with these feminine duties, Frederick was proving a successful soldier. On 22 April he joined Mansfeld in the Lower Palatinate, to the great joy of his beleaguered subjects, and on 27 April they won a victory at Mingolsheim over the forces of the Catholic League, under Count Tilly. That night Frederick slept again in the castle of Heidelberg, where he and Elizabeth had enjoyed such peaceful, happy years together at the start of their married life.

His military good fortune was, however, short-lived. Soon Elizabeth was writing regretfully to 'Honest fat Thom' Roe : 'The prosperity the King hath had in the Palatinate did not last long, for he was constrained to leave his army, being ready to mutiny for lack of payment.' King James of England, still putting his trust in treaties, bade his son-in-law retire from the field of battle, and with an ill will Frederick obeyed.

From Sedan, where in happier days he had been educated under the care of his guardian the Duke de Bouillon, he wrote despondent letters to his wife at The Hague. 'Would God there were a little corner of the world where we might live happily together, that is all the happiness I ask!' he sighed. As an afterthought he added, somewhat petulantly, 'But living at The Hague does not agree with me at all.' Greater trials were to follow. In September Christian of Brunswick – 'who hath engaged himself only for my sake in our quarrel', as Elizabeth put it – was badly wounded in battle and lost an arm. Then, after a siege lasting eleven weeks, Heidelberg finally fell to Spinola. 'Voilà, my poor Heidelberg is taken,' Frederick wrote sorrowfully to Elizabeth. 'They have used all sorts of cruelties, pillaged the whole town, burnt all the suburbs which were the chief beauty of the place.' He lamented, 'Certainly if I were to follow my inclination, I should retire from it all and leave the King of England, for the good of his children, to do what he should think best for them.' He had some more harsh words to say about the unpleasantness of living at The Hague, 'among such people', but he was glad to learn that his ally Christian was recovering from his amputation, 'for certainly I would rather lose an arm myself than that he should die'. There were little items of family news and loving messages interposed among the politics. 'Little Rupert is very clever to understand so many languages,' he commented, and he concluded his letter adoringly, 'Continue to love your poor Celadon always, and rest assured that his thoughts are continually with his soul's star.'

Early in October 'poor Celadon' returned to The Hague from Sedan. Elizabeth's pleasure in having her husband beside her again was tempered by the gloom of their situation. Frederick was so changed in appearance that she fainted when she first saw him, and the weeks which followed brought no news to comfort her. On

5 November Sir Horace Vere was obliged to surrender Mannheim; now all that remained to Frederick of the fine country that had been his was the solitary fortress at Frankenthal, Elizabeth's dower town. Frederick's 'distemper and passion' when the news of the fall of Mannheim was brought to him were alarming; Elizabeth bore the blow more stoically, with 'watery eyes and silence'. Sir Dudley Carleton, the English ambassador at The Hague, who was her constant friend, observed sympathetically, 'God send them both patience.'

Another old friend who invoked God's assistance for the distressed couple was John Donne, now Dean of St Paul's. He sent the exiled Winter Queen the text of a sermon which he had recently preached before her father and Elizabeth replied with a charming letter of thanks.

Good Doctor D., You lay a double obligation on me; first in praying for me, then in teaching me to pray for myself, by presenting to me your labours. The benefit likewise I hope to be double, both of your prayers and my own, and of them both to both of us; and as I am assured hereof (though it hath pleased God to try me by some affliction) so I desire you to be of my thankfulness unto you, and that I will remain ready upon any good occasion, to express as much as lies in the power of Yours & c., Elizabeth.

Early in 1623 Elizabeth learned to her surprise that her prayers were urgently required on another's behalf. The news which reached her from England in February was startling; it appeared that her much-loved younger brother, the Prince of Wales, accompanied by her father's favourite, the Duke of Buckingham, had set out in disguise to pursue his courtship of the Infanta of Spain in person. It was a hazardous and foolhardy undertaking. King James had burst into tears and tried to persuade his 'Baby Charles' and 'Sweet Steenie Gossip' not to expose their precious persons to such dangers, but the young men were eager to go. Travelling incognito as 'Jack and Tom Smith' they set off from Dover, and made their way to Madrid via

Paris. Elizabeth was 'much afflicted with the apprehension of the Prince's journey'. She found some comfort in the fact that the Spanish were unlikely to harm Prince Charles, since in the event of his death she would become the next Queen of England, but the news of her brother's adventure clearly upset her. She feared for his religion as well as his safety. In her anxiety she became indiscreet; she confided too much of her feelings to 'a certain lady of the highest rank' in England. Damaging rumours spread that the exiled Queen of Bohemia was preparing to come to England, to be ready to claim her rights if her brother should fall victim to the Spanish, or, still more sinister, that she was about to send her eldest child over. 'For God's sake preach more wariness to the Queen,' her friend Lady Bedford begged Sir Dudley Carleton. Old age had made King James more fretful and suspicious than ever; he lived in constant dread of plots and treason, and the last thing he wanted during his heir's absence was his daughter's inflammatory presence within his kingdom.

In fact Elizabeth, who was pregnant once again, had no intention of travelling to England at this time. Resentful though she and Frederick undoubtedly were of her father's attitude to their political and personal misfortunes, they remained obedient to his wishes. In April 1623 they made an arrangement which showed that they expected their stay in hospitable Holland to be a long one. The Prince of Orange had graciously given them the use of one of his lesser residences, in the university town of Leiden, and here they decided 'to settle the three children they have here', as it was reported, 'under the government of M. de Plessen and his wife, both persons very fit for such a charge'. One reason for the decision was said to be the smallness of their own house for such a large and growing family, but in later years Elizabeth's youngest child was to give her own tart explanation for her mother's decision. 'Her Majesty had her whole family brought up apart from herself,' she wrote, 'preferring the sight of her monkeys and dogs to that of her children.' To the nursery palace at Leiden went Frederick Henry, Rupert and the baby Louise, to be joined later by Charles Louis, the little Elizabeth and Maurice, from Berlin.

The woman who could be accused of finding her pets more amusing than her children was also the woman of spirit and courage who wrote to Sir Thomas Roe that spring : 'Though I have cause enough to be sad, yet I am still of my wild humour to be as merry as I can in spite of fortune.' It was a gallant attempt at cheerfulness, since, as she told him in the same letter, 'All grows worse and worse,' and went on, 'My father will never leave treating, though with it he had lost us all.' Frederick, instead of being a support to her, was at times a severe cause of worry. Ever subject to moods and depressions that were the very opposite of Elizabeth's buoyant optimism, he was becoming increasingly unpredictable. The King of England's latest bout of 'treating' with Spain and Austria by which he was endeavouring to secure the return of the Palatinate for his son-in-law and daughter provided for a fifteen-month truce in the Palatinate; 'the conditions are very hard – to be so long without succouring his poor subjects, as fifteen months, and at the end of all, not certain then to do it; but the king my father's will to us is law which we will ever obey in that we can,' Elizabeth wrote to Lord Conway. Frederick, despite his bounden obedience to his father-in-law's will, could not resist reminding him that he had promised to supply him with ten thousand soldiers in return for his retiring from the Palatinate as he had duly done in the previous year. In the middle of June, Frederick suddenly felt he could bear it all no more; taking a disquietingly passionate leave of his wife, and telling her only that he was off on an afternoon's jaunt to Schevening, to try out the wind-carriages, he disappeared for several days and nights. It was feared that he must have gone off on some wild venture with Christian of Brunswick. When at last a letter arrived informing Elizabeth that he had taken himself on an art-tour of Amsterdam and Haarlem, the queen's fears were set at rest, but loyal Sir Dudley Carleton betrayed something of his annoyance at the king's behaviour when he commented that Frederick seemed these days to be more liable to run away than to fight.

The troublesome treaty remained to be signed. Frederick was shocked by one of the provisions which stated that he must disown

95

his allies, halt their efforts on his behalf, and recognize the emperor's enemies as his own. To abandon such loyal comrades-in-arms as Christian of Brunswick seemed to him the height of dishonour – and little remained to him but his honour. Eventually, however, he was prevailed upon to sign. 'I hope his majesty is pleased with the king, who hath, to obey his command, signed the treaty,' Elizabeth wrote, somewhat bitterly. Christian of Brunswick demonstrated his continuing friendship for Frederick by attending a banquet given in honour of the Winter King and Queen at Delft but his presence proved something of a dampener to the occasion, since he appeared very gloomy and was seen to sigh frequently.

On 21 August Elizabeth gave birth to her seventh child. It was another boy. This baby, born amidst the uncertainty and unhappiness of 1623, was to be the first of her children to die in infancy. He was given the name of Louis, in hopeful compliment to the King of France, but he was too delicate to undergo a formal christening ceremony for many weeks.

The Duke of Buckingham was one of those invited to stand as godparents to the new baby. A Spanish agent in London circulated a rumour that still closer ties between Buckingham and the family of the Winter Queen were proposed, and that a marriage was being planned between Elizabeth's eldest son, Prince Frederick Henry, and Buckingham's daughter. With the object of setting King James against Elizabeth, the agent also gave it out that she had sent her secretary, Sir Francis Nethersole, to Spain with the intention of breaking off the Prince of Wales's match with the infanta. Furious, Elizabeth roundly denied both stories, calling them 'two of the greatest lies that could have been invented'. She told the King of England plainly that she had written the infanta a letter of goodwill, solely to please him, and had sent her the best pair of earrings she could afford 'in the condition I am in'. As for the second accusation, 'I protest that I never had any thought of it.' She could not say openly what was plainly the case – that the daughter of the jumped-up Duke of Buckingham was no fit bride for the King of Bohemia's eldest son.

Buckingham and Prince Charles had returned from Spain dis-illusioned and displeased with the Spanish. Urged on by his 'sweet boys', the aged and increasingly feeble King James summoned, in February 1624, what was to be the last Parliament of his reign. 'One thing gives me much hope of this Parliament,' Elizabeth wrote optimistically to Sir Thomas Roe, 'because it began upon my dear dead brother's birthday.' She added the happy news, 'I must also tell you that my brother doth show so much love to me in all things, as I cannot tell you how much I am glad of it.' In his opening address to his last Parliament, King James dwelt on the subject of the Palatinate; he told the assembled members that he had hoped to preserve his name of 'rex pacificus', and die in peace like an aged Simeon, but that he could not do so while his daughter's rights remained unrestored. He went on to pledge his support for war, should it prove necessary. Parliament, eager for war with Spain, which, it was generally assumed, would involve the restoration of the Palatinate as a matter of course, voted the sum of £300,000 to pay for it.

It seemed for a time that the distressed Lady Elizabeth could look for an improvement in her fortunes in 1624. The unreliable soldier in her cause, Count Mansfeld, made the journey to England to offer his sword, and was greeted with enthusiasm not only by Buckingham and Prince Charles, but by the crowds of Englishmen who flocked to greet him as he rode through the streets. Ironically, the count was lodged in the very apartments in St James's Palace which had recently been fitted up for the arrival of the Prince of Wales's Spanish bride.

It was becoming increasingly certain that Charles would now, in place of the infanta, have a French princess for his wife. During their brief sojourn in Paris, 'Jack and Tom Smith' had caught sight of the little Princess Henrietta Maria practising her dancing in the Louvre. Elizabeth learned that it was this rather plain fourteen-year-old who was to become England's next queen. Her choice of a present to send her brother's future mother-in-law Marie de Médicis was charac-teristic: she looked around for a suitable little dog to please her. The Winter Queen had reason to welcome the French marriage, since one of the terms of the marriage-treaty was to be aid from France in the restoration of the Palatinate.

On 6 October Elizabeth gave birth to another son, who was given the name of Edward. This happy event was followed shortly afterwards by a tragedy : on Christmas Day the sickly Prince Louis died. 'It was the prettiest child I had,' Elizabeth wrote sadly. Having safely borne so many handsome, healthy sons and daughters she seemed bewildered by the death of this little boy; she told Thomas Roe that she had never lost a child before, and professed herself surprised that he could have died, as it appeared, from teething troubles.

'There is great strife 'twixt love and death/Which of them is the stronger,' a Jacobean poet had written at the time of her brother Henry's death. The conflict of love and death was to become painfully familiar to Elizabeth as the years passed. Not long after she had buried Prince Louis, she learned that she herself was now an orphan. On 27 March 1625, James I died at Theobalds. 'You may easily judge what an affliction it was to me to understand the evil news of the loss of so loving a father as his late Majesty was to me,' Elizabeth wrote to Lord Conway. No doubt she did feel a pang at the death of her father, but her grief at his passing was clearly outweighed by her pleasure in the accession of Prince Charles – 'so dear and loving a brother as the King is to me, in whom next God I have now all my confidence', she wrote.

King Charles I came to the throne of England filled with good intentions towards his sister and brother-in-law. Frederick willingly renewed the solemn undertaking which he had previously given James I – that he would be guided by his will. England appeared to be making ready for war; when the Spanish asked why, Charles answered with dignity that the Queen of Bohemia now had a king for a brother. But Charles had inherited an empty exchequer; he had no money for great military enterprises. Buckingham, who was as disliked by Parliament as he was admired by the new king, was blamed for mismanagement. And while Charles and his Parliament wrangled, Mansfeld's troops went hungry and unpaid. Once again, Elizabeth's hopes were to be disappointed.

In the autumn of 1625 the great Duke of Buckingham paid a visit to The Hague. Having fallen out with both the Spanish and the French factions in England, he now sought the support of the Puritans, and to this end he thought it politic to demonstrate a personal friendship with their adored Queen of Bohemia. Officially he went to The Hague to seal an alliance between England, Denmark and Sweden with the States-General, but privately he had another reason for making the journey. He hoped to bring about the very match which Elizabeth had hotly repudiated when it was rumoured during the previous year. The rich, powerful Duke of Buckingham, the handsomest man in England and intimate of two Stuart kings, saw no reason why his well-dowered little daughter should not be allied with the eldest son of the exiled, penniless Winter King. During his stay he went to Leiden to see Elizabeth's children, and struck up a friendship with Frederick Henry, who was now a clever and attractive boy of eleven. As Charles's influential confidant, Buckingham was a man with whom Elizabeth thought it wise to maintain good relations, but she had no intention of marrying off her heir, third in line to the throne of England, to the daughter of an upstart, even one as dazzling as the duke.

1626 was another dark year for the Winter Queen. It opened promisingly enough with the occupation of Lower Saxony by her uncle, King Christian iv of Denmark, who had now entered the war, but in June her admirer and Frederick's valuable comrade-in-arms Duke Christian of Brunswick died. She was about to give birth to her ninth child; normally her confinements were remarkably easy, but this time she had a long and difficult labour. She was in low spirits for some time following the birth of the baby girl, who was christened Henrietta Maria in honour of the new Queen of England. 'We were fain to christen the girl in haste, she was so sick,' Elizabeth wrote. Her sister-in-law, who was still childless, accepted the compliment graciously. In August King Christian of Denmark was defeated at the Battle of Lutter by Count Tilly, and forced to abandon most of Lower Saxony, and then at the end of the year Mansfeld died;

he was no great personal loss, but the course of the war now seemed more uncertain than ever.

In spite of the mounting pressures of debt and disappointment, Elizabeth regained her customary cheerfulness, and took an interest once more in a building project. A summer palace at Rhenen, on the Rhine, was to be constructed for the pleasure of the Winter King and Queen. For once Frederick could lay his hands on some money; in 1623 he had sold the town of Lixheim and invested the proceeds for his children, and the interest on that capital sum was sufficient to allow him and his wife to indulge their taste for building on a modest scale. At Rhenen Frederick would be away from 'the canaille of the Hague' which he disliked so intensely, and there Elizabeth could hunt to her heart's content. The expense seemed worthwhile, and the artistic Charles I took an interest in the plan.

Elizabeth was at Rhenen during the summer of 1628 when the handsome, hated Duke of Buckingham met his death at the hands of a fanatical assassin named John Felton, who stabbed him to the heart, crying, 'God have mercy on thy soul.' Though Buckingham had never been one of her intimates, the exiled queen was startled and shocked. 'The Duke of Buckingham's death did breed no small wonder here,' she wrote to Lord Conway. 'I am sorry for it, and specially to have him die in such a manner so suddenly.' She went on to say that she found no small comfort in the knowledge that her brother the king would continue to take great care 'in those affairs that concern me'. With Buckingham out of the way, she hoped that Charles and his subjects might come to a better understanding.

Neither age nor anxiety seemed to impair Elizabeth's childbearing abilities. As she entered her thirties her regular pregnancies continued; in September 1627, her tenth baby was born. A fine healthy boy, he was given the name of Philip, and the States of Utrecht and Gelderland acted as the sponsors at his christening. With such an abundance of sons and daughters to her credit, Elizabeth appeared scarcely to miss the two who remained far away in Berlin. Perhaps she preferred to forget Prince Maurice, the baby she had borne amidst the miseries of her flight from Prague; at all events, she never set eyes on him from the time of his birth until he was eight years old. It was not until 1628 that he and his sister Elizabeth, the eldest daughter, were sent from Berlin to join the royal nursery establishment at Leiden. Charles Louis had arrived some time before, but then he was the acknowledged favourite, 'even when he was but a second son'. It was difficult to account for Elizabeth's preference, since the heir, Prince Frederick Henry, was a clever and engaging child, with royally great expectations. The early years of King Charles 1's marriage proved childless; if Henrietta Maria failed to produce a family of her own, the Winter Queen's eldest son would one day inherit the throne of England. There were many loyal Englishmen who devoutly hoped that it would happen. To the growing Puritan faction, a child of the beloved Lady Elizabeth would be more welcome as King of England than any son of the French Papist who shared Charles Stuart's bed.

With the assent of his all-important English uncle, it was declared that the fourteen-year-old Prince Frederick Henry would soon be old enough to join the army of the Prince of Orange as a volunteer in the war against Spain, as his father had before him. Before this plan could be put into action, however, a tragedy as great as any which had previously befallen Elizabeth occurred. What began as an exciting pleasure-trip for a father and his young son turned into a disaster which was to plunge the family of the Winter Queen into grief and shorten Frederick's own melancholy life.

The sad affair began with the news of a most welcome windfall for Elizabeth. On behalf of the West India Company, prizes had been captured in which Elizabeth had a share, left to her and Frederick in the will of Prince Maurice of Orange when he died in 1623, to be succeeded by his brother Henry. The fleet and its booty lay at anchor in the Zuider Zee, and by all accounts it was a fine sight; Frederick and his eldest son decided excitedly that they would go and see it for themselves. On 7 January 1629, they set off in high spirits, leaving Elizabeth still recovering from the birth of her latest baby, the ailing Princess Charlotte. The boat which the Winter King and his son took to Amsterdam was over-full of eager sightseers, but Frederick chose not to waste money on obtaining private transport – perhaps he thought it would be good for his son to rough it a little, in preparation for his soldiering career. It was a fatal decision. When the accident happened just outside Amsterdam in the fog, and a heavy vessel crashed into the frail boat with its royal passengers, most of the people floundering in the icy waters could not be saved. The sailors' first thought was for the King of Bohemia. He was rescued. His son, whose most treasured christening gift had been a crystal ship, was drowned. His frozen body was found next morning, clinging fast to the mast of the wrecked boat.

Frederick was too helpless with grief to break the news to his wife. The task fell instead to her old friend the former Lord Doncaster, now Lord Carlisle, whom in happier times she teased with the nickname of 'Camel's face'. The shock of the announcement almost killed Elizabeth, it was reported, yet with her customary courage she rallied, and set about the terrible task of consoling the distraught Frederick. Charles I had to provide the bereaved family with money for mourning clothes, and he tried to help with the pathetic business of deciding where the child should be buried. The parish church near the Wassanaer Hof was considered unsuitable for the Bohemian king's half-Stuart heir, even as a temporary measure until a grave could be found for him in Heidelberg or Westminster Abbey, but King Charles's suggestion that the boy might lie next to his infant brother Prince Louis at Delft had to be overridden, on the grounds of expense. Eventually Prince Frederick Henry was interred in the Cloister Church of The Hague.

Letters and messages of sympathy for the tragic couple poured in from all quarters. 'I do easily believe your affliction on the loss of my poor boy, which I cannot but think of still,' Elizabeth wrote gratefully to the Earl of Essex in March. Her friends were worried by reports of the Winter King's health; she tried to allay rumours that the tragedy had left him seriously ill. 'Indeed he was never well since; but I hope all is past,' she wrote in the following year to loyal Sir Thomas Roe. She explained : 'The King here hath been evil first of a sore throat and since of a weakness which took away his stomach, but after that an impostume or two broke out upon his body he is well again and I hope will be abroad at Easter.' She did not want her friends to worry too much; 'I write this to you because I know you will hear many rumours of his sickness that may make you afraid,' she told her 'Honest fat Thom'.

In search of solace she and Frederick fled to Rhenen, where building work on their many-windowed Italianate palazzo was well under way. Here Elizabeth could try to forget her unhappiness in a relentless round of riding and hunting. Frederick did not stay long, however; action was, as ever, his cure for melancholy, and in the summer of 1629 he once again joined the army of the Prince of Orange. Whatever Elizabeth might protest in her letters, her husband was not in good health either physically or mentally after his son's death and his own narrow escape from drowning. Unknown to Elizabeth his physician's private opinion, which reached the ears of the King of England, was that the exiled Winter King could not be expected to live long.

Birth, rather than death, was on King Charles's mind as the year 1630 opened, however. His temperamental French wife was at last pregnant, and on 29 May she fulfilled his hopes by giving birth to a healthy son – a baby as dark as her sister-in-law's children. The prince was named Charles. It now seemed that the Winter Queen and her children would never inherit the throne of England; in The Hague, Frederick and Elizabeth made a point of demonstrating their pleasure in the event, and gave a celebration banquet. Frederick accepted the honour of standing sponsor to his newborn nephew. The birth of a twelfth child and fifth daughter to Elizabeth in October seemed, by comparison, unimportant. That this last little girl was, against all the odds, to be the mother of a King of England and found a lasting dynasty could scarcely have been anticipated at the time. Her parents had even run out of names by the time she was born, and, as she herself recorded in after years, 'The plan was adopted of writing various names on slips of paper and casting lots for the one which I should bear; thus chance bestowed on me the name of Sophia.'

The newest baby remained unchristened for several months, for her sister Charlotte died on 23 January 1631, after a long and languishing sickness, and she had to be buried before the baptism could take place. The dead infant was finally laid to rest next to her brother Prince Frederick Henry, in the Cloister Church at The Hague. Burying her children was becoming an all-too-familiar experience for the distressed Winter Queen.

During the year 1630 a former suitor of Elizabeth's re-entered her life – this time in a blaze of triumph, as the champion of the Protestant cause. Gustavus Adolphus, King of Sweden, had proved to be a good and successful peacetime ruler; during the 1620s, in campaigning successfully against the Poles, he had had the opportunity to demonstrate the outstanding skills which were to make him one of the greatest military commanders in history. Now he undertook the invasion of Germany with a large army. Typically Scandinavian in appearance, he was tall, blond-haired and blue-eyed, with a ruddy complexion, and the Italian mercenaries nicknamed him 'The Golden King'. Certainly he seemed to have a golden touch in matters of warfare. For Frederick and Elizabeth, who had grown accustomed to disillusionment, faint hope turned to incredulous delight as town after town fell to the new hero. News of victories for their side made a welcome change for the exiled king and queen at The Hague.

Like his father before him, though for different reasons, Charles I of England was putting his trust in treaties to bring about the restoration of the Palatinate. To Elizabeth's concern, he was once again involved with negotiations with Spain. 'By treaty it will never be done, as you may easily see by the delays they have already made; and let yourself not be deceived,' she wrote worriedly in the autumn of 1631, somewhat to her brother's annoyance. He considered himself to be doing what he could in military terms by permitting another of Elizabeth's champions, the Scots-born Marquis of Hamilton, to raise seven thousand troops at his expense with which to fight alongside the King of Sweden – an enterprise which Charles could not be seen publicly to countenance, for fear of damaging his delicate relationship with Spain. Elizabeth was afraid that without

strong support from England Gustavus Adolphus might 'be disheartened to do anything for us, and make his own peace, so as we
shall never have anything, but live to be a burden to you and a grief
and affliction to ourselves and posterity', as she told her brother. To
Thomas Roe she complained a few months later that she and
Frederick were being treated 'as little children that cannot keep
counsel, for when we desire to know what is treated, we are answered
that it is not fit that such things should be divulged abroad'.

The truth was that where Elizabeth's father had been unwilling,
her brother was unable to provide the desired military aid for her
cause. The King of Sweden requested that Charles I should supply
twenty-five thousand soldiers and agree to maintain them for four
years; it was a demand far beyond the King of England's means.
Gustavus's opinion of Frederick's situation was summed up in his
pitying comment, 'A brother of the King of Great Britain and
protected by the States, and must he come to me in his doublet and
hose? Let him come, howsoever, and I will do my best to restore him
to his patrimony.' In the middle of January 1632, Frederick duly set
out from The Hague to join the Swedish champion in the field.

He did not depart until he had put his family affairs in order. He
pawned a large amount of plate, and withdrew another considerable
sum from the proceeds of the sale of Lixheim. He compiled careful
inventories of his belongings, and, as though he had some presenti-
ment, he wrote to Charles I, entrusting Elizabeth and his children
to the King of England's care. And he delayed his departure until he
had seen his newest child christened.

On 2 January Elizabeth had given birth to her thirteenth and last
baby. It was another son. Frederick was pathetically anxious to give
this infant prince the names of the dead Frederick Henry, but as
usual political considerations prevailed, and the little newcomer was
baptized after the all-important Gustavus Adolphus. The ceremony
took place on 13 January, in the Cloister Church where the two
children who had died young lay buried.

On 16 January, his business completed, the Winter King said
farewell to his wife, and set out on his journey. One of those who

went with him was a slight, fair young Englishman named Lord Craven. Fabulously rich, the son of a Lord Mayor of London, William Craven had forsaken the comforts of his life in England to fight for the Protestant cause as a commander in the Marquis of Hamilton's little army. Elizabeth and he had conceived a lasting friendship; with the absent Gustavus Adolphus he had stood sponsor to her new baby, and throughout his life he was to be one of her most devoted and generous supporters, pledging his wealth and risking his life in her service. It was a curious coincidence that Craven should also have been the new owner of Elizabeth's childhood home, Combe Abbey.

Travelling through difficult weather conditions, the Winter King made a brief halt at Leiden, where he took leave of his brood of children. The Swedish soldier-king whom he was journeying to join was to remain a lifelong hero to at least one of Frederick's young sons – Prince Rupert, himself destined to win fame as a soldier, studied Gustavus Adolphus's tactics with zeal, and later put his cavalry methods to good use in the English Civil War.

At seven o'clock in the morning of 11 February the exiled King of Bohemia met the victorious King of Sweden for the first time, at Hochst. Elaborate compliments passed between them, and Gustavus Adolphus made a point of treating Frederick with the greatest possible courtesy, calling him 'mon frère' and ostentatiously acknowledging his kingly rank. Nothing in his demeanour towards the Winter King revealed his true opinion of the worn-out failure who was now his brother-in-arms.

The people of the beleaguered Palatinate received their former ruler with every sign of genuine joy, running out to see him and welcoming him 'with infinite expressions of joy and contentation'. Only three fortresses now remained in enemy hands – Kreuznach, Frankenthal, and Elizabeth's early married home of Heidelberg – and these seemed likely to be re-conquered before long by the victorious Swede. Kreuznach fell soon after Frederick's arrival. Lord Craven distinguished himself at the siege, and although wounded was first into the breach. Once again it seemed as if Elizabeth had grounds for hope.

As usual Frederick missed his wife badly and wrote to her constantly. The Queen of Sweden was with her husband, and Frederick wished Elizabeth might join him; he assured her that when the situation looked more secure he would send for her, 'although, to tell you the truth, at the moment I see little sign of it'. He began his letters 'Dearest heart', and assured her, 'My thoughts are always with you, whom I love with all my heart.' On another occasion, when she had offered to send him the proceeds of a small inheritance which King Charles had lately forwarded to her, Frederick wrote tenderly, 'I would wish you to have this inheritance and invest it, and thereby pay off your debts bit by bit, wanting nothing from you but that you love me always as much as I love you. You may be very sure that no absence will ever cool my love, which is truly perfect.' Time and misfortune had done nothing to diminish the love which had begun in such promising circumstances twenty years earlier. 'Since he went from hence he never failed writing to me twice a week, and ever wished either me with him or he with me,' Elizabeth was to recall wistfully after his death.

As the year 1632 progressed the hopes of the Winter King and Queen fluctuated. 'Good M. de Plessen is fortunate to be dead,' Frederick wrote morbidly in March. For all his good actions on behalf of their cause, Gustavus Adolphus made it plain that he did not intend to restore Frederick to his dominions for some time. Frankenthal and Heidelberg had yet to be recaptured, and the important question of the rights of the Lutherans in the Palatinate remained to be resolved. When Frederick proposed to raise his own independent army the Swedish king objected. 'It was not secure to have more than one chief,' as Lord Craven put it. 'I do not know what I am about,' Frederick complained to Elizabeth. 'I see very well that the King of Sweden does not intend that I should have troops.' He went on morosely, 'I do not know therefore what I shall be good for, or why the King of Sweden desired me to come.' The devastation of the Palatinate was another source of grief to the exiled ruler. 'I arrived on Tuesday at Oppenheim, which does not at all resemble what you saw; the house is in ruins and half the town burnt,' Frederick told Elizabeth. His morale was very low.

At The Hague Elizabeth kept herself busy. Family affairs took up a good deal of her time : Charles Louis, the favourite and now the heir, had smallpox; there was a new governor to be appointed at Leiden, following the death of M. de Plessen; there were little portraits to be painted and sent to Frederick. And she had a constant correspondence, on matters both personal and political, to maintain. On one occasion her diplomatic skills were brought to bear on a dispute which had arisen between the English ambassador Sir Henry Vane and the King of Sweden. 'I know that he himself was sorry for it after that his choler had passed,' Elizabeth wrote soothingly to Vane. 'I pray make the best of all, and remember his good actions, and forget his words.' The Winter Queen would have made a far more able statesman than her husband; as Charles I once commented bluntly of his sister and brother-in-law, 'The grey mare is the better horse.'

On 6 November the Protestant hero Gustavus Adolphus, on whom Elizabeth and Frederick had placed so much hope, was killed at the Battle of Lützen. The day resulted in a notable victory for their side, but the death of the Swedish champion was a crushing blow. He was found stripped naked beneath a pile of dead bodies, covered in wounds. It was a dark day for the Protestant cause. Elizabeth had once observed that misfortune seemed to pursue those who were her friends; it was a sad fact that many of those who had fought in her cause had died, from Christian of Brunswick and Count Mansfeld to the great King of Sweden.

Frederick never recovered from the death of Gustavus Adolphus. Ever since his own narrow escape from drowning he had been in poor health; now he contracted the plague. It seemed he no longer had the will to live, and on the morning of 19 November, 1632, at the age of thirty-six, he died. He had achieved virtually nothing in his short life; a high-principled, dutiful nonentity, he had been cast in a role which he had neither the ability nor the personality to play successfully. A man cut out for comfortable domesticity, he had been obliged by circumstances to take on the part of a Protestant hero, and the results had been disastrous both for himself and for Europe. Only in his private life, in his passionate and enduring love for his fascinating wife, had he achieved any distinction : in her eyes he was a great man, and his death was the worst blow of her tragic life.

When Dr Rumph brought the news to Elizabeth at The Hague she became almost literally senseless with grief. 'It was', she later wrote, 'the first time ever I was frighted in my life.' For three days she could not weep. She did not eat, drink or sleep, and she did not speak a single word. 'It pains my heart to see her in this state,' the Princess of Orange's mother wrote to Sir Henry Vane, with anxious sympathy. To King Charles of England Elizabeth described herself, a month later, as 'the most wretched creature that ever lived in this world'; pathetically, she went on, 'And this I shall ever be, having lost the best friend that I ever had, in whom was all my delight; having fixed my affections so entirely upon him that I should have longed to be where he is, were it not that his children would thus have been left utterly destitute.' Charles's immediate reaction to the tragic news was to invite his sister to come to England at once. It was a generous proposal, and Elizabeth must have longed to return to the secure, welcoming country of her happy childhood. With a delicate sense of propriety she refused, however, deferring to the etiquette of her married home – 'the custom in Germany being not to stir out of the house for some time, after such a misfortune. And since I was married into this country I should wish to observe its customs carefully.' There was a yet stronger reason for her wishing to remain where she was : now that Frederick was dead, the rights of the heir Charles Louis remained to be fought for. 'I put no small constraint on my inclinations in not obeying your commands to come to you; for God knows that it would be my only comfort,' she wrote, 'but I must prefer the welfare of my poor children to my own satisfaction.'

For all Frederick's shortcomings, Elizabeth had loved him whole-heartedly, and her grief at his death was overwhelming. The misfortunes of the 'distressed Lady Elizabeth' were now complete; as she wrote to Sir Thomas Roe, five months later, 'Though I make a good show in company, yet I can never have any more contentment in this world, for God knows I had none but that which I took in his company.'

CHAPTER SEVEN
Family Fortunes

In London it was rumoured that the Winter Queen had died of grief. 'The Queen's affliction is greater than anyone can imagine,' the Princess of Orange's mother told Sir Henry Vane, and the English ambassador at The Hague, William Boswell, wrote, 'Whether the Queen will long be able to bear the grief thereof, they who are nearest about her do much doubt.' But those who expected Elizabeth to give way, even under such a weight of misery, misjudged her. She had too much courage and strength of will to break down, however great the stress, and in this moment of near despair she was supported by her sense of duty towards her fatherless children. 'The last request that their father made me, before his departure, was to do all that I could for them; which I wish to do, as far as lies in my power, loving them better because they are his than because they are my own,' she wrote to Charles I.

After lying for several days 'petrified with grief' in her black-hung chamber, Elizabeth prepared to face the world again. In the words of one of her attendants, she emerged from the ordeal 'the greater for her trials'. Her first visitor was the Prince of Orange, whose presence gave her great comfort. In England an official deputation was being assembled, headed by the Earl Marshal, Lord Arundel, and including her old friend the charming rogue Lord Goring; they arrived on 2 January 1633, and were shown into her presence without delay.

It was to England that Elizabeth and her young family now looked for comfort – 'after God, our sole resource is in you', the widow wrote to her brother. At Leiden her four eldest sons took upon themselves the solemn task of writing to their English uncle to ask for his protection.

Sir, In this great affliction which God hath laid upon us all, we see no hope of comfort or relief, but from your gracious majesty; for God hath taken from us our dear lord and father, and in him the care of us all. Hitherto we have been brought up by your bounty and now are fit subjects of your compassion. The enemies of our father deceased are the enemies of our House, which they would quickly destroy, if your majesty forsake us. Therefore we commit ourselves, and the protection of our rights, into your gracious arms, humbly beseeching your majesty so to look upon us, as upon those who have neither friends nor fortune, nor greater honour in this world, than to belong unto your royal blood. Unless you please to maintain that in us, God knoweth what may become of Your majesty's most humble nephews and servants Charles Rupert Maurice Edward.

England was for these boys, as it had been for their grandfather King James, the Promised Land. In Rupert and Maurice, the image of the king at Whitehall inspired a loyalty which made them willing to risk their lives in his service.

It was hoped for some time after Frederick's death that his widow might return to London; arrangements for her voyage were drawn up and her old lodgings known as the Cockpit were made ready for her. Elizabeth was adamant, however, and even Lord Arundel's deputation could not persuade her to return to her former home, since it might seem to her enemies that she was abandoning the long struggle for the Palatinate. She was determined to remain where she was and fight, by every means in her power, for her eldest son's rights. As she later wrote apologetically to Archbishop Laud, 'All I fear is you will think I have too warring a mind for my sex; but the necessity of my fortune has made it.'

At Leiden the formal routine of the children's life continued much as before. In later years the vivacious Princess Sophie recorded her memories of daily life at the nursery establishment.

We had a court quite in the German style. At ten o'clock the dancing-master was always welcome, for he gave me exercise until eleven, which was the dinner-hour. This meal always took place with great ceremony at a long table. On entering the dining-room I found all my brothers drawn up in front, with their governors and gentlemen posted behind in the same order side by side. I was obliged by rule to make first a very low curtsy to the princes, a slighter one to the others, another low one on placing myself opposite to them, then another slight one to my governess, who on entering the room with her daughters curtsied very low to me. I was obliged to curtsy again on handing over my gloves to their custody, then again on placing myself opposite to my brothers, again when the gentleman brought me a large basin in which to wash my hands, again after grace was said, and for the last and ninth time on seating myself at table.

The constant pressures of debt and disinheritance had not prevented Frederick and Elizabeth from making sure that their children were properly brought up.

With the sad exception of the youngest, the fair-haired Gustavus, who was epileptic, Elizabeth's ten remaining sons and daughters were a credit to her. The Stuart family had an inherited tendency both to exceptional height and exceptional shortness; unlike their diminutive uncle Charles I, Elizabeth's sons grew very tall. They were a handsome, high-spirited and talented family, with far more of their mother than their ineffectual father in them. Princess Elizabeth was a serious, clever young woman, who became a close friend of the philosopher Descartes; Princess Louise, an engagingly unconventional girl who always looked as if her clothes had been thrown on her, painted with unusual skill. Princess Henrietta was pretty and domesticated, with a fondness for cooking sweet things, and little Princess Sophie, destined to be the ancestress of kings and queens, was a sharp, observant, quick-witted child. Rupert, who acquired the colourful nickname of 'Rupert le diable', had an unusual range of talents; he had a natural flair for languages, he drew superbly, he was interested in scientific experiments, he was an outstanding sportsman whom Samuel Pepys in after years described as one of the best tennis players in England, and from an early age he was fascinated by all things military. In Rupert, Elizabeth had bred a son who was a natural leader, and Prince Maurice, who came next to him in age, followed him devotedly in war and peace until his early death.

It was clearly the destiny of Elizabeth's sons to become soldiers. They had little alternative. 'I think he cannot too soon learn to be a soldier in this active time,' the Winter Queen wrote of her favourite, Charles Louis, in the spring of 1633; with her blessing he set off to join the army of the Prince of Orange. Rupert was only thirteen at this time, but it was said that he already handled his arms with the skill of an experienced officer, and he was eager to put his boyhood training into practice, so his mother allowed him to join his elder brother in the field. His first experience of active service was a marked success, and he made an excellent impression on the seasoned campaigners who observed him.

'Here she liveth for her children's sake, in whom is all her joy,' Elizabeth's secretary wrote to Sir Thomas Roe in February 1635, 'although I remember when you passed once by in Leyden, the sight of them made your eyes to water.' Poverty, bereavement and uncertainty dogged the Winter Queen and her family, and yet their high spirits seemed irrepressible. In the same month as her secretary wrote pityingly to Roe, 'God's blessing be ever with them, for they must support their house, since their house cannot support them,' the distressed queen's fatherless children were putting on a ballet of hunters for their mother's amusement, to the accompaniment of much laughter and wild 'hallooings', all of which greatly shocked a group of visiting Puritans.

1635 was the year when Charles Louis had his eighteenth birthday and officially came of age. Elizabeth decided that he should make the journey to England and plead his cause in person with his uncle;

loving her glib-tongued eldest son as she did, she did not doubt that he would make an excellent impression on Charles I and his court. 'He is young and very inexperienced, so as he will no doubt commit many errors,' she wrote deprecatingly, privately confident that the boy's charm would make up for his lack of sophistication. She was not disappointed; her friends returned polite reports of the young Palatine's progress. Elizabeth was emboldened to try a more daring experiment and send her next son, Prince Rupert, after his brother. This time her reservations were genuine. Rupert was not only gauche, he could be extremely wilful, and in her eyes he lacked the attractive qualities of the favoured Charles Louis. 'I hope for blood's sake he will be welcome,' she wrote uncertainly, and added, 'I believe he will not much trouble the ladies with courting them, nor be thought a very beau garçon which you slander his brother with . . . he is still a little giddy, though not so much as he has been.' To her astonishment, the forthright Prince Rupert quickly overshadowed his elder brother, and became far more popular. 'Certainly he will réussir un grand homme, for whatsoever he wills, he wills vehemently,' wrote Sir Thomas Roe. 'His majesty takes great pleasure in his unrestfulness, for he is never idle, and in his sports serious, in his conversation retired, but sharp and witty when occasion provokes him.' If King Charles was delighted with the boy, so was Queen Henrietta Maria; to Elizabeth's grave disquiet, she did all she could to convert him to Catholicism. When an exotic scheme to make him governor of Madagascar was proposed and caught the public imagination, Elizabeth was horrified; she compared it to one of Don Quixote's ventures, and called it 'a thing neither feasible, safe nor honourable for him'. There was, she pointed out, 'work enough to be had for him in Europe'. Charles Louis did not hesitate to fuel his mother's fears for Rupert's religious welfare, and she became increasingly anxious to get him away from England and the dangerous influences of the Stuart court. She gave the excuse that she wished him to rejoin the Prince of Orange's army; 'he will spend this summer better in an army than idle in England, for though it be a great honour and happiness to him to wait upon his uncle, yet, his youth considered,

he will be better employed to see the wars.' Anxiety for her sons
safety in battle never seemed to enter Elizabeth's head. 'The Prince o
Orange is preparing to go speedily into the field and I mean to send
my third son Maurice with him to learn that profession which
believe he must live by,' she had written in May. As events were to
show, in Elizabeth's eyes Rupert's religion mattered as much as hi
life.

'You may easily guess why I send for him, his brother can tell i
you; I pray help him away as soon as you can, and hinder all you
can those that would stay him,' she wrote to Sir Thomas Roe. In the
summer of 1637 Prince Rupert returned to The Hague. Hunting
with King Charles on the morning before his departure he announced
with characteristic impetuousness that he wished he might break hi
neck, so that he might leave his bones in England. For the young
Rupert of the Rhine this happy visit had laid the foundations of a
love of England which was to last throughout his life.

If Elizabeth's sons were expected to become soldiers, it seemed that
her daughters' destiny must be marriage. During the absence of
Charles Louis and Rupert, the King of Poland had shown a gratify-
ing interest in the blue-stocking Princess Elizabeth. She had grown
into a beautiful, high-minded and clever young woman, and her
relationship to the King of England was not the least of her attrac-
tions. Vladislav of Poland hoped that as the nephew by marriage of
King Charles I he would be able to count on English support for his
attempts to regain the throne of Sweden which his father had lost
some forty years earlier. Elizabeth did not welcome the match. The
Swedish throne had passed to Christina, the orphaned daughter of
Gustavus Adolphus, and the exiled Winter Queen was shocked at
the idea that any member of her family should help to disinherit the
child of their dead champion. Vladislav was, in any case, not an
attractive suitor for a young girl, since he was a middle-aged widower
with a penchant for women; and there was a major obstacle in the
fact that Elizabeth would evidently have had to change her religion
in order to become his queen. This was naturally out of the question
for a daughter of Frederick and Elizabeth of Bohemia. The

dispossessed queen's attitude to the matter was characteristic: 'For myself,' she wrote, 'if it be found good for my son's affairs, and good conditions for religion, I shall be content with it; else, I assure you, I shall not desire it, my son being more dear to me than all my daughters.' Elizabeth's marriage, like everything else, must take second place to Charles Louis's interests and the restoration of the Palatinate.

Early in 1636 Lord Arundel was sent to the emperor to discuss the latest terms for Charles Louis's restoratio... .. was proposed in Vienna that Frederick's heir should be permitted to repossess the Lower Palatinate and that he should be married to a daughter of the house of Habsburg. When Arundel talked to Elizabeth about the conditions he found her opposed to them; she was particularly upset to think of her son marrying the emperor's daughter, who was much older and reputed to be very unattractive. More importantly, she did not believe Charles Louis should be fobbed off with half measures. 'If he accept of a little he will never have more,' she wrote. 'I am for tout ou rien.' She told Archbishop Laud, 'I do not think he will be restored fully otherwise than by arms; sixteen years makes me believe it.' The archbishop gently chided her for her warlike attitude, and in a subsequent letter Elizabeth apologized for seeming both un-Christian and unfeminine, but she pointed out, 'I remember never to have read in the chronicles of my ancestors that any king of England got any good by treaties, but most commonly lost by them, and on the contrary, by wars made always good peaces. It makes me doubt the same fortune runs in a blood, and that the King my dear brother will have the same luck.' Eventually the negotiations broke down, and Elizabeth and her son became more anxious than ever to obtain active support from Charles I.

'It seemeth to me as a dream, and makes me fear it is too good a purpose, and too happy, to come to an issue,' Charles Louis wrote to his mother in January 1637. The reason for his excitement was a promising change in his circumstances: King Charles had agreed to lend him a fleet and to permit him to raise soldiers from among his English supporters. 'My lord Craven hath already offered me ten thousand pounds for his share,' Charles Louis reported happily. By the autumn of 1638 the young elector had raised a force of some four thousand soldiers; accompanied by his brother Rupert and the ever-generous Lord Craven, he set out for the front. The Emperor Ferdinand III had reaffirmed his father's actions by confirming that the Upper Palatinate belonged to Maximilian of Bavaria; it was clear that if Charles Louis was to recover his hereditary possessions, it must be by force of arms.

On 17 October, at Vlotho, the Palatine's force, under the command of the Scotsman General King, faced a far larger body of Austrian troops under Count Hatzfeld. Their little army was put to flight. Charles Louis dexterously retired from the battlefield; Lord Craven was wounded· Rupert, fighting furiously, was cut off from his men and taken prisoner. Asked who he was he replied belligerently, 'A Colonel.' Colonel Lippe struck up his helmet, and said with surprise, 'Sacramet, it's a young one!' He was quickly identified as the Queen of Bohemia's son and taken away to captivity.

Elizabeth's anxiety over the fate of her soldier sons was made the more painful by the lack of reliable information as to the whereabouts of the young prisoner-of-war. 'If I were sure where Rupert were, I should not be so much troubled,' she wrote to Sir Thomas Roe. She went on : 'If he be prisoner, I confess it would be no small grief to me, for I wish him rather dead than in his enemies' hands.' When the news finally reached her she was gravely troubled. 'Rupert's taking is all,' she told Sir Thomas Roe. 'I confess in my passion I did rather wish him killed. I pray God I have not more cause to wish it before he be gotten out.' The most pressing danger now was that the boy's captors would prevail on him to change his religion, to the detriment of Charles Louis's interests. As soon as he could, Rupert sent word to his mother that 'neither good usage nor ill should ever make him change his religion or party', and Elizabeth took some comfort from his assurances. 'I know his disposition is good, and he never did disobey me at any time, though to others he was stubborn and wilful,' she wrote. 'I hope he will continue so, yet I am born to so much affliction that I dare not be confident of it, and

James I by Daniel Mytens, 1621

Anne of Denmark, attributed to W. Larkin

ABOVE LEFT Elizabeth, attributed to
Paul van Somer

ABOVE RIGHT Henry, Prince of Wales,
attributed to Robert Peake, *c.* 1610

LEFT Charles I as Duke of York by
Robert Peake, *c.* 1610

OPPOSITE ABOVE Combe Abbey,
Warwickshire

OPPOSITE BELOW Visscher's Long
View of London, 1616

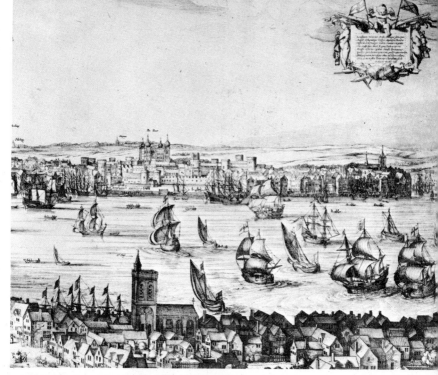

Frederick of Bohemia
by G. Honthorst

The arrival of Frederick
with Elizabeth at
Flushing in May 1613
(detail: the *Prince Royal*)
by Hendrick C. Vroom

Heidelberg in the early seventeenth century by
Matthew Merian

The Elector Frederick on the Wheel of Fortune,
from a German print, 1621

Prague in 1649 by Wenceslaus Hollar

Charles Louis in 1637 aged 19
by François Dieussart

Prince Rupert, studio of
Van Dyck, c. 1637

Princess Sophia by 'F.M.R.', 1648

The Earl of Craven, attributed to
Princess Louise

The Hague in the mid-seventeenth century

Queen of Bohemia.

Elizabeth by G. Honthorst, 1642

this affliction had not been to be suffered, but that I am comforted that my sons have lost no honour in this action, and that him I love most is safe.' As Rupert prepared to face a long captivity in the lonely fortress of Linz, steadfastly refusing all inducements to make him change his religion, it was as well that he was not aware of his mother's blithe, cruel comment, 'Him I love most is safe.'

As it turned out, the favourite was himself to have a taste of prison life in the near future. He planned to join forces with the army of Duke Bernard of Saxe-Weimar, but found himself forestalled; on his way through France he was summarily arrested and sent to Vincennes on the orders of Cardinal Richelieu — 'this ulcerous priest', Elizabeth called him vituperatively. The pretext was that Charles Louis was travelling illegally without a passport; the fact was that Richelieu did not wish him to gain control of the army. She did not believe that any harm would come to her eldest son, 'but the loss of time and the affront is all'. She informed Sir Thomas Roe that Richelieu's attachment to the house of Austria was the reason for his action, and that Charles Louis's chief fault was the fact that he was the King of England's nephew. The younger princes, Maurice, Edward and Philip, had been sent to Paris to finish their education and acquire some French sophistication; they too were confined, though their detainment proved to be of shorter duration than that of Charles Louis, who was obliged to spend seven months under guard. Eventually Charles Louis accepted his captors' terms; he agreed not to leave France without permission and to renounce his intention of joining the army of Saxe-Weimar. Elizabeth was not altogether happy to learn that her son had accepted these terms, but she excused him on the grounds that 'necessity hath no law'.

Rupert was not so lucky. He was obliged to spend three years of his youth in lonely confinement, often under unnecessarily heavy guard. While he was at liberty he had wavered in his religious convictions; now, under duress, he was stalwart. The governor of his prison 'importuned him to go to the Jesuits. He answered no, except he might also go elsewhere.' The governor then proposed 'that he would receive their visits. He answered no, except other persons

119

E

might also be allowed to come to him.' Plans for an escape were clearly futile, though Elizabeth entertained romantic schemes for some time, and at one moment Maurice advanced near enough to Linz with Swedish troops to allow her hopes to rise. For the energetic and impetuous Rupert the enforced idleness of prison life must have been very hard to bear. With a resourcefulness such as Elizabeth might have shown, he did what he could to relieve the tedium of his days; when not permitted to play handball, shoot with a 'screwed gun' or 'ride the great horse', he occupied himself by drawing and limning and working on Dürer's theory of perspective. The English ambassador Lord Arundel presented him with a big, thick-coated standard poodle puppy, who was to remain his faithful companion and become notorious in Roundhead propaganda until it was killed on the battlefield of Marston Moor. The dog, whom he named 'Boy', was not the prince's only pet. He also had a tame hare, who slept on his bed; when his door was unbolted in the morning, 'the hare would leap down off the Prince's bed and go open it with her mouth'. As usual Elizabeth's second son greatly impressed those who met him. The Archduke Leopold, brother of the emperor, came to see him and treated him with great kindness; after that Rupert's captivity was considerably eased, and he was allowed out on parole to pay short visits to neighbouring nobles, which made a pleasant change for the lonely prisoner.

Loyal Sir Thomas Roe negotiated tirelessly for his release. Late in 1641 it came at last, on the condition that Rupert would never again take up arms against the emperor. On the advice of Charles I, Rupert accepted the terms. He went in person to take leave of the emperor, his family's hereditary enemy, and was hospitably entertained; his imperial host benignly advised the young prince not to risk travelling through the territory of the warlike Duke of Bavaria, and instead Rupert made his way home through Bohemia. No doubt he was curious to see the colourful country where he had been born, and his parents had enjoyed their one brief year of majesty.

On a cold night in December Sir William Boswell, ambassador at The Hague, was leaving the Queen of Bohemia, who had just sat down to her supper, when he was surprised to see a carriage draw up in the courtyard. Out leapt Prince Rupert, tired and travel-stained, but happy, having arrived home much sooner than expected. 'Your lordship will imagine what joy there was,' Boswell wrote to Sir Thomas Roe. Elizabeth was overjoyed to see her second son again; in her opinion he was not changed, 'only leaner and grown'. The years at Linz had left their mark, however. After his long captivity the active-minded Rupert urgently needed an outlet for his pent-up energies and frustrated abilities. He was to have it all too soon.

In England, as Rupert was aware, the conflict between king and Parliament was coming to a head. Charles I's enforced concessions, which included the execution of his friend and counsellor Lord Strafford, had achieved next to nothing, and his bungled attempt to arrest the five members of Parliament whom he considered to be his chief opponents was tantamount to a declaration of war. It was becoming tragically obvious that the King of England would soon be in a position to give employment to his soldier nephews.

Early in the spring of 1642 his spirited queen, Henrietta Maria, arrived in Holland, after a terrible crossing. She had come to help the war effort by selling jewels and buying arms, but the official reason for her visit was given out as family business. She was accompanied by her elder daughter, the Princess Mary, who was now the wife of William, eldest son of the Prince and Princess of Orange – somewhat to the chagrin of Charles Louis, who considered that he himself should have had the honour of marrying the King of England's senior daughter. He had been passed over, however, in favour of the fifteen-year-old son of the Prince of Orange and his wife, who, to add insult to Charles Louis's fancied injury, had formerly been Elizabeth's lady-in-waiting. Now the ten-year-old Mary was on her way to join her young husband at her father-in-law's court, under the watchful care of Henrietta Maria.

Elizabeth of Bohemia and Henrietta Maria had little in common and reason enough to be jealous of one another, but they gracefully established a cordial relationship, in spite of their opposing religions. Elizabeth's youngest daughter, Sophie, who was of an age to be a companion to the new little bride, narrowly appraised her celebrated French aunt, and later wrote down her impressions. She found Henrietta Maria far less beautiful than Van Dyck's portraits had led her to expect, and described her as 'a little woman with long lean arms, crooked shoulders and teeth protruding from her mouth like guns from a fort'. However, she was found to have lovely eyes, an elegant nose and a beautiful complexion, and when she was heard to say that the Winter Queen's youngest girl somewhat resembled her own daughter, Sophie was so flattered that from then on she considered her 'quite handsome'. As a rather plain, brown-skinned child, Sophie hankered for compliments; she was further gratified when she overheard some of the English gentlemen in her aunt's train remark that when she grew up she would eclipse all her sisters. 'This remark gave me a liking for the whole English nation,' Sophie recorded artlessly.

Elizabeth was more guarded in her reactions to the English visitors. 'I hear all and say nothing,' she wrote to Sir Thomas Roe. She did, however, comment that the little Frenchwoman and her followers held very belligerent attitudes to the troubles in England. 'I find by all the Queen's and her people's discourse that they do not desire an agreement between his Majesty and Parliament, but it all be done by force,' she told 'Honest fat Thom'. Regrettable as it was that Charles I's wife was not a peacemaker, her martial spirit was to stand her in good stead, since she was to face considerable personal dangers in the ensuing war.

In August 1642, Rupert and Maurice sailed for England. After a brief encounter with a Parliamentary cruiser which fired on their ship off Flamborough Head, they arrived safely and joined King Charles at Nottingham, where the royal standard was raised on 22 August. Rupert was made General of the Horse, and he quickly established himself as an immensely able and popular commander. After his first action of the war, at Powick Bridge, where he routed a force of Parliamentary horse, he became the Cavaliers' hero, as adored by the Royalists as he was vilified by the Parliamentarians. In Roundhead propaganda his dog 'Boy' was described as a devilish cur, and his chattering female monkey – probably a present from Elizabeth – was depicted with an obscenity which was ill-suited to the godly Puritan authors. Eventually, against his better judgement, Prince Rupert was prevailed upon to reply to the enemy's stream of slanders against his character and actions. Having roundly rebutted the accusations of 'barbarousness and inhumanity' to women and children, he went on to defend his uncle the king against charges of Roman Catholicism, pointing out 'what a gracious supporter hath he been in particular to the Queen of Bohemia (my virtuous royal mother) and to the Prince Elector my royal brother'. As for his own religious sympathies, he declared proudly, 'And for myself, the world knows how deeply I have smarted and what perils I have undergone for the Protestant cause.' The long imprisonment at Linz was still all too fresh in his mind.

'The people's goodness alone made them give to the Queen of Bohemia so many great and free contributions,' announced the sharp rejoinder to Prince Rupert's 'Declaration'. The anonymous pamphlet went on, 'You have not only taken away their wills but their means of ever doing the like; having brought us to so wretched a condition that we shall never hereafter have leisure to pity her, but rather consider her as the mother of our calamities.' Elizabeth's traditional position as the heroine of the Puritans in England had been badly shaken by her sons' participation in the Civil War. Some letters written by her to Prince Rupert were intercepted, and the allowance of £12,000 a year on which she depended for her livelihood promptly ceased, 'which doth trouble me very much', she wrote agitatedly to Sir Thomas Roe. In her opinion it was most unjust of Parliament to deprive her of her money, when there was nothing she desired more than 'the public peace and good of the kingdom'. On 13 April 1643 she wrote to the Speaker of the House of Commons, saying winningly, 'I cannot be at rest until I have endeavoured to remove all such impressions as might deprive me of their [the Commons'] good opinion which I so truly value.' She explained that she could not quite remember what she had written in her letters, 'but if anything did perchance slip from my pen, in the private relation between a mother and a son, which might give them the least distaste, I entreat them to make no worse construction of it than was by me intended'. She ended by imploring the House 'to take my pressing wants into their kind consideration'.

With her customary forthrightness she discussed the problem in her letters to Sir Thomas Roe. She told him she knew that certain people were claiming she had urged Rupert and Maurice to go to her brother, which, she insisted, 'is very false, as for Maurice you know I wished him somewhere else, but I neither could nor would hinder them from going, seeing the King desired them'. This brought her to the touchy subject of Charles Louis. Whilst her younger sons had been brought up in the knowledge that it would be their destiny in life to fight for another's cause, Charles Louis had, ever since he became the heir, been taught to regard his own rights as being of paramount importance. He had accordingly grown into a supremely self-seeking young man. Despite the ties of blood and his debt of gratitude to his uncle, he had declined to fight for King Charles, and had actually left his side when war broke out and returned to The Hague. From there he gave his support to the Parliament side. If they should win, and the king be overthrown, there was every chance that they might look to the Queen of Bohemia's half-Stuart and wholly Protestant eldest son to be the country's new leader. Elizabeth was reluctant to censure her beloved Charles Louis, but she was clearly disappointed in his behaviour. 'I confess I did not much approve the fashion of my son's leaving the King because I thought his honour somewhat engaged in it,' she explained to Sir Thomas Roe. 'If he had not been then with the King I would not have counselled him to go to him, but being there I thought it not much to his honour to leave him at that time.' Mindful of her own need of Parliament's good will, she added hastily, 'God knows not out of any disaffection to the Parliament, but my tenderness of his honour, and desire that he might not lose my brother's affection.' Philosophically, she closed the subject by saying, 'He is now of age to govern himself and choose better counsels than mine are, and so I leave him to them, not meaning to meddle with them.' Elizabeth was now in

her forty-seventh year; she was resigning herself to the role of
dowager.

Conscious of the harm which Rupert's activities on behalf of the
king were doing to his family's standing with Parliament, Charles
Louis was anxious to exculpate himself and his mother from all
responsibility for his brother. As he wrote to Sir Thomas Roe, 'It is
impossible either for the Queen my mother or myself to bridle my
brother's youth and fieriness.' He added firmly: 'It will be a great
indiscretion in any to expect it, and an injustice to blame us for
things beyond our help.'

While she tried to maintain a neutral stance in public, Elizabeth's
private loyalties lay with her brother the king. The news of her
family which reached her from England during the year 1643 was,
for the most part, heartening. After the inconclusive Royalist victory
at the Battle of Edgehill, in October 1642, the Cavaliers had enjoyed
a series of successes, and they owed much of their good fortune to the
energy and bravery of Prince Rupert. 'In truth, he hath a flying
army,' commented one contemporary news-sheet; it seemed that the
prince had the power to be in several places at once, recruiting,
besieging, advising. A colourful mythology began to grow up around
him. He acquired nicknames – 'Prince Robber' and 'The Bloody
Prince' unjustly among them. Stories of his duping the Roundheads
by going among them in disguise were circulated, and the God-
fearing enemy were quick to accuse him of devilish practices, casting
'Boy' the dog in the role of his familiar. To his own men the young
prince was a hero, however. In July 1643 he successfully stormed
Bristol, with the help of his faithful brother Maurice, and thus the
king was once again in possession of one of the country's major
ports. 'Long may you live a terror to your uncle's enemies and a
preserver of his servants,' wrote the Earl of Newcastle, early in
August. In Rupert the Winter Queen had a son to be proud of.

'Youth and fieriness' were, however, still the prince's besetting
weaknesses. Some of the king's counsellors resented the intervention
of this high-handed, half-foreign young general in the affairs of the
kingdom, and his military advice, which was generally very sound,

was constantly disputed. There was no doubt that Rupert had built up the king's troopers into first-rate cavalry, but the very force of their thundering charges was a drawback; they proved difficult to control, and were liable to gallop off the battlefield in pursuit of the fleeing enemy instead of wheeling to return to the thick of the fighting. Their defeat at Marston Moor, in 1644, at the hands of Lieutenant-General Oliver Cromwell, marked the turning-point for Prince Rupert's forces.

1644 was a difficult year for Elizabeth. She no longer enjoyed the robust health of her youth, and she began the year with a bad attack of pleurisy. Her spirits were brought down by the death of her mother-in-law, the old Electress Louisa Juliana, and then in the summer one of her oldest and dearest friends, the indefatigable Sir Thomas Roe, also died. In one of her last letters to 'Honest fat Thom', Elizabeth told him worriedly, 'I have yet little hopes of getting of the Parliament those moneys that are due to me, I cannot imagine why they should be so hard to me, I am sure I do not deserve it except it be a fault that I am the King's sister which is a crime I shall never be sorry for.' In the absence of regular payments from Parliament she continued to suffer from 'pressing wants'; her credit with the patient tradesmen of The Hague was running out.

During the following year Elizabeth had further anxious communications with the Speaker of the House of Commons on the subject of her money. Parliament had, in her words, 'been pleased to vote several orders, and thereby declare a purpose to provide for my supply', but still no cash was forthcoming. 'The creditors here were fed with expectations to receive something every month, but now, after so many months, their hopes fail them and my debts increase,' she wrote desperately. Not until she had taken the step of sending over her chaplain, whom Parliament had officiously appointed for her, were her revenues forwarded to her.

The end of 1645 brought news of two disturbing events. In England Prince Rupert fell out with his uncle. His surrender of Bristol was the cause of the rift; unjustly, Charles I declared that he would rather see a son of his knocked on the head than that he should do 'so mean an action'. Rupert was summarily deprived of his command and sent a passport to go 'somewhere beyond seas'. The prince demanded a court-martial and was exonerated of all blame; eventually Charles made an official declaration that his 'right dear nephew' was 'not guilty of any the least want of courage or fidelity to us, or our service, in that action'. The relationship between king and prince had been severely strained, however, and Rupert was a disillusioned man.

The other source of distress for Elizabeth was her fourth son, Prince Edward. So far none of her attractive, impecunious sons and daughters was married, although there had been various tentative negotiations. An enormously rich young Frenchwoman, Mlle de Rohan, had been proposed as a bride for Prince Rupert. As Charles Louis pointed out with a nice sense of priorities, she was 'great both in means and birth, and of the religion'. When the fiercely independent Rupert made it clear that he had not the slightest intention of getting married, King Charles had written a charming letter to the next of the brothers, beginning, 'Nephew Maurice, Though Mars be now most in vogue, yet Hymen may sometimes be remembered,' and asking 'if you will not by your engagement take your brother handsomely off'. Despite the inducement of the lady's fortune Maurice had followed his brother's example in this as in everything else, and refused the offer. Thus it was that Prince Edward became the first of Elizabeth's children to marry, which he unexpectedly and distressingly did, at the end of 1645.

It was a secret love-match, contracted while he was in Paris; what made it almost unbearable for the Winter Queen was the fact that the bride was a Roman Catholic, and Edward had changed his religion to marry her. Her name was Anne de Gonzague, and she was a daughter of the rich Duke de Nevers, several years older than Edward and extremely sophisticated. She had fallen madly in love with the penniless but exceptionally handsome young prince and succeeded in winning him over to Rome. Elizabeth was distraught at the news. She declared to Charles Louis that she wanted to die, at which her eldest son piously advised her to remit all to God's providence. No doubt making the mistake of judging his brother by himself, he told her that he did not believe Edward's conversion to be sincere. 'He cannot be so easily persuaded of those fopperies which he pretends to, having been so well instructed in the contrary.' He feared that his erring brother's new-found allegiance to Rome would conflict with his obedience to his mother. The most pressing need, now that Edward could not be saved, was to safeguard the next son, Philip, from falling into similar evil hands and his attendants were subjected to careful scrutiny. When Philip was about to go and serve with the Venetian army in the spring of 1646, Charles Louis advised Elizabeth that at parting she should, along with her blessings, 'lay your curse upon him, if he changes the religion he hath been bred in'.

As it turned out, Philip was indeed to fall from grace but in quite a different way. His offence was murder; his motive, his mother's honour. A French gentleman at The Hague named Jacques de l'Epinay had for some time been a close friend of Elizabeth's. She treated him with unusual familiarity, so much so that scandal-mongers began to gossip excitedly, linking his name with those of Elizabeth and her daughter Louise. Charles Louis was in England with his Parliament friends at the time, and the rest of the brothers were scattered abroad; only the eighteen-year-old Prince Philip was on hand to defend the honour of his house. Outraged that his mother's reputation should be called into question through the pre-tensions of an upstart foreigner, he exchanged high words with de l'Epinay. Contemporary opinions as to what followed differed, but the fatal upshot was that the hot-headed prince waylaid de l'Epinay in the street by night and stabbed him to death with his hunting-knife. The boy then fled the country.

He had acted rashly, but in the opinion of Charles Louis, the head of the family, there was a good deal of excuse for what he had done. He wrote to his mother from England to intercede on his brother's behalf. 'Give me leave to beg your pardon in my brother Philip's behalf, which I should have done sooner, if I could have thought that he needed it,' he wrote. 'The consideration of his youth, of the affront he received, of the blemish had lain upon him all his lifetime if he had not resented it; but much more that of his blood, and of his nearness to you, and to him whose ashes you have ever professed more love and value than to anything upon earth, cannot but be sufficient to efface any ill impressions which the unworthy representation of the fact, by those who joy in the divisions of our family, may have made in your mind against him.' There was more than a suggestion of reproof for Elizabeth in Charles Louis's letter; he implied that his mother should have shown more care for her reputation. 'I hope I am deceived in what I hear of this, and that this precaution of mine will seem but impertinent, and will more justly deserve forgiving than my brother's action,' he wrote. His letter concluded, 'I will still be confident that the good of your children, the honour of your family, and your own, will prevail with you against any other consideration.' The scandal had been considerable but Prince Philip was never brought to justice, fortunately for his family. Instead, he became the only one of Elizabeth's sons to die in battle, at Rethel in 1650, aged twenty-three.

1648 was a momentous year for Elizabeth. The appalling war which for almost thirty years had ravaged Germany was drawing to an end; a part of the hereditary domains which her husband had lost was about to be restored to her son. On 27 October the Peace of Westphalia was signed in Münster. 'I am for tout ou rien', Elizabeth had once written proudly, but after three decades of bitter fighting it was a much depleted patrimony which Charles Louis finally received. The Upper Palatinate remained in the hands of Maximilian of Bavaria, as did the all-important title of First Elector of the Empire. An eighth electorate, the most junior of all, was specially created for Elizabeth's son. At least he would repossess Heidelberg – but it was a Heidelberg much battered and defaced. The peaceful, prosperous setting of Elizabeth's early married life was sadly changed, and its population had been decimated. However, the longed-for restoration had come at last, and Elizabeth and her family could not but rejoice at the change in their fortunes.

It was ironic that within weeks of this triumph their joy was overshadowed by mourning. As had happened thirty-five years before, at the time of Elizabeth Stuart's wedding, her happiness was blotted out by the death of a brother. On 30 January 1649, King Charles I stepped out of the Banqueting House where Elizabeth's betrothal had taken place and with regal dignity met his death before the eyes of his gaping subjects. Elizabeth was stunned and appalled. All celebrations had ceased abruptly when it became known that her brother was on trial for his life; rumour had it that the exiled Queen of Bohemia was about to set sail for England. She had one shred of comfort – Charles died in the knowledge of her love. 'Her affection truly speaks her my sister,' he wrote warmly in one of his last letters. The disappointing behaviour of Charles Louis was amply compensated for by the stalwart loyalty of the king's two younger nephews; when Charles set out in disguise from Oxford in 1646 to go to the Scots, Rupert had begged to accompany him, and was only dissuaded on the grounds that his exceptional height would betray his identity. To the end, Rupert had been tireless in his uncle's service, even dreaming up plans for his escape. To Elizabeth, the death of Charles I was both a family tragedy and a national disaster, and to the end of her days she wore a mourning ring bearing the initials C.R. under a crowned skull and crossbones, and containing a faded lock of his hair. As the last surviving member of James I's family she took her responsibilities seriously.

Cromwell and Parliament were from then on anathema to her. There was no question of maintaining her public stance of neutrality; she let her detestation of her brother's murderers – 'those devils' – be known to the world. Her household were forbidden to associate with the English ambassadors at The Hague, on pain of being thrown bodily out of doors. To her satisfaction, her son Prince Edward publicly insulted the 'pretended ambassadors'; Elizabeth commented that he had done no more than call them by their true names. Parliament responded by playing its trump card: her pension was stopped. She called on the States-General to intercede for her, but, predictably, their efforts met with no success. Elizabeth found herself in worse financial straits than ever; as her youngest daughter, Sophie, later wrote gaily, 'We were at times obliged to make even richer repasts than that of Cleopatra, and often had nothing at our court but pearls and diamonds to eat.' Even Frederick's beautiful engagement ring eventually found its way into pawn.

To Elizabeth's disappointment, Charles Louis did not share her attitudes; even after the execution of Charles I he remained friendly with Parliament. Reproached by his mother for not writing to Queen Henrietta Maria, he replied stiffly, 'Until the King and Parliament were agreed, I being with the Parliament, it was not fit nor safe I should keep correspondence with her.' He added characteristically, 'I had very good cause to believe that my letters would not only be unacceptable, but also would be made use of to my prejudice.' He did, however, handsomely 'resolve to write to her Majesty', to please his mother, and he reminded her that he had done some harm to his reputation among his friends in England by seeing Charles II and refusing a meeting with Parliament's agent at The Hague.

Though her son refused to identify himself with the cause of her martyred brother, there were others who showed an impressive loyalty to the House of Stuart. Early in 1649 Elizabeth met for the first time the great soldier James Graham, Marquis of Montrose; the queen and the general quickly became close friends.

> He either fears his fate too much
> Or his desserts are small
> Who dares not put it to the touch
> To win or lose it all,

ran one of Montrose's most famous verses; it was a philosophy with which the resolute Winter Queen would entirely have concurred. There was no suggestion of a romance between them; Sophie later wrote that Montrose had hoped to marry the artistic Princess Louise. But Elizabeth Stuart and 'Jamie Graham' had much in common besides their Scottish birth, and they corresponded on a note of relaxed familiarity. When a deputation of commissioners from Scotland requested Elizabeth to help persuade her nephew Charles II to give himself up to their guidance she wrote to Montrose about it, adding as a postscript, 'I give you many thanks for your picture, I have hung it in my cabinet to fright away the Brethren.' Her last letter to the hero whom she teasingly called 'wicked Jamie Graham' wished him safety in Scotland. Her hopes were not fulfilled. Montrose was defeated and hunted down as an outlaw, and on 21 May he was hanged, drawn and quartered in Edinburgh. Sophie wrote that she was deeply shocked on hearing that the gallant Montrose had been put to a cruel death; her mother's feelings may be imagined.

By the end of the 1640s there had been a curious reversal in the fortunes of Elizabeth's family. Now it was the King of England who was in exile, while the young Elector Palatine was restored to his father's former home at Heidelberg. The time had come for Charles Louis to marry and beget children to succeed him; early in 1650 his wedding took place. It was an eminently suitable alliance. The new Electress Palatine was a descendant of William the Silent and a devout Protestant, named Charlotte Elizabeth of Hesse-Cassel. The Princess Sophie, who went to stay with her brother and sister-in-law at Heidelberg, left an illuminating account of their relationship. Charlotte Elizabeth was decidedly odd-looking, with flaxen hair and dyed black eyebrows, but she lost no time in informing Sophie that she had had many suitors, and had married Charles Louis against her will, a revelation which shocked the daughter of the loyal and loving Winter Queen. The elector was equally anxious to confide his grievances; he told Sophie that his wife had been badly brought up, and asked the girl to do what she could to cure her of 'all her affectation'. In spite of all this fault-finding, the couple were constantly kissing and embracing in public, and Sophie was embarrassed by their habit of frequently kneeling to one another.

While Sophie was at Heidelberg her eldest sister, Elizabeth, and her brother Edward were also staying with the head of the family. The younger brother and sister were greatly disappointed in Elizabeth. She had always been studious, but since the death of her dear friend and mentor the philosopher Descartes, she had become much changed, both in mind and person. Prince Edward whispered to Princess Sophie, 'Where has her liveliness gone? What has she done with her merry talk?' To Sophie's annoyance, her sister became very bossy with her and factions began to develop in the stately castle where Frederick and Elizabeth had once known such happiness. The Winter Queen's eldest daughter never married. In her early forties she entered a Protestant convent, and eventually she became an abbess. To the lively Sophie, hers was an unenviable fate.

Princess Henrietta, the prettiest of the family, became the first of the Winter Queen's daughters to marry. Her wedding took place in the spring of 1651; her husband was Prince Siegmund Rakoczy, brother of the Prince of Transylvania. It was an honourable alliance, and Henrietta wrote glowing letters describing her new family and home. It appeared that she and her husband had fallen in love. But tragedy followed. The fair-haired spring bride had always been delicate; she died in the autumn. Her husband was inconsolable, and he did not long survive her. To the end of her life, the Winter Queen retained tender memories of 'my poor Henriette'.

1651 was a year of birth, as well as marriage and death. 'I had from my Lord Craven the birth of your son, and was a little surprised you did not write it to me,' Elizabeth wrote to Charles Louis, on 14 April. 'I wish you all happiness with your boy.' Relations between the Winter Queen and her eldest son had considerably deteriorated, and their letters were now taken up with financial wrangling; she could not send her new little grandson a present, she wrote, 'for truly all my jewels almost are at pawn, only such left that I cannot give away, keeping them for your father's and my eldest brother's sake'. Elizabeth was at first surprised by Charles Louis's attitude; 'I did not think that I should be put to dispute with you for my maintenance,' she told him in the summer of 1659, and went on to remind him of all that she and her friends had expended on his behalf in the past. 'I am not so unreasonable as to think that you have the same revenues out of the lower Palatinate as the King had,' she informed him, but added imploringly, 'I cannot live upon the air.' To Prince Rupert she wrote, 'Though I am not so unreasonable as to ask all my jointure because I know your brother cannot give it, yet I may justly ask more than he gives me.' Charles Louis wanted his mother to come and live at Heidelberg, thus saving the expense of two separate households, but Elizabeth was reluctant. No doubt she remembered her own feelings about having her mother-in-law living at Heidelberg during her own early married life; she knew that there were 'crotchets' within the elector's establishment 'which in several kinds are very troublesome', as he discreetly put it, and she had no wish to strain still further her relationship with her eldest son. Charles Louis was very pressing on the subject, which annoyed her. 'I believe he means to starve me out of this place, as they do blocked towns,' she complained to Lord Craven. 'I know he may do it, and has already begun pretty well; but he will have as little comfort as honour by it, for if I will be forced by ill usage to go, I shall be very ill company there.' Charles Louis's response sounded considerate, but it contained a note of grievance; 'I know your majesty hath no reason to long for to be here, considering the great change you will find in all things ... and the small confidence your majesty hath in my endeavours or power to please you.' In the summer of 1655 the States-General made her a subsistence allowance of a thousand guilders a month, 'till I shall be able to go from hence, which God knows how and when that will be, for my debts'. Until her creditors had been settled with, and her 'many little piddling debts', as well as the greater ones, seen to, she could not depart from The Hague. 'If you would add but what you did hint, you would do me a great kindness by it, and make me see you have still an affection for me,' Elizabeth wrote on 13 August. Times had changed since Charles Louis was the adored favourite who could do no wrong.

It was the forthright, unconciliatory Prince Rupert who had turned out to be the best of Elizabeth's sons. 'As for Rupert you need not trouble yourself,' she wrote stiffly to Charles Louis in 1650, 'we understand one another very well.' She wished fondly that he were nearer home, but she understood and approved his adventurous course of life, spent in the service of the Stuarts. His soldiering done, Prince Rupert embarked on a new career, which called upon yet another of his varied talents – that of seamanship. He became admiral of the exiled Charles II's little fleet, with his devoted brother Maurice as his second-in-command. Their mission was to combat the forces

of Parliament at sea as they had on land. The meagre five-strong
Royalist fleet was ill-provided; the Winter Queen pawned some
more of her few remaining jewels to help fit it out. 'Misfortunes
being no novelty to us, we plough the sea for a subsistence, and being
destitute of a port, we take the confines of the Mediterranean Sea for
our harbour; poverty and despair being companions, and revenge our
guide,' wrote the keeper of Rupert's log. Privateering and the taking
of prizes became the Cavalier princes' way of life; where once Rupert
of the Rhine had led horsemen thundering across the English
countryside, he now bore down on the enemy under sail in the blue
waters of the Mediterranean, or wherever he and his squadron met
with ships friendly to the Commonwealth. Spanish merchantmen
were fair game, since Spain was not opposed to the English Government. The King of Portugal, on the other hand, proved a useful
friend to Rupert and Maurice : offering all the assistance his kingdom could afford them, he gave shelter to the fleet and hospitality to
the princes. Admiral Blake proceeded to blockade them in the Tagus,
and for a time a sea-battle between the forces of king and Parliament
seemed imminent. There was an attempt to kidnap Rupert while he
was out hunting; he retaliated by trying to plant a bomb on board one
of Blake's ships. These were exciting times for Elizabeth's adventurous younger sons.

On one occasion Prince Rupert nearly drowned. In bad weather
his ship, the *Constant Reformation*, sprang a leak, and began to sink;
neither the *Swallow* nor the *Honest Seaman* could get close enough
to take her sailors off. 'Prince Maurice, bearing under his stern, and
being sadly sensible of his brother's ruin, was not apprehensive of
his own, but commanded his master to lay him aboard, resolving to
save his brother or perish with him,' ran the stirring account in the
log. 'The Princes endeavoured to speak one to another, but the
hideous noise of the winds and seas overnoised their voices.' It
looked as though Rupert was about to go down with his ship, but
there followed an extraordinary act of gallantry. 'His men, seeing
supplications would not prevail', launched the only lifeboat, 'and by
force put him into it, desiring him at parting to remember they died

F

his true servants'. During the Civil War Prince Rupert had earned the reputation of being 'shot-free'; though he constantly ran great risks, he seemed to bear a charmed life. Now, once again, he had cheated death.

Prince Maurice did not share his brother's miraculous luck. In September 1652, in a hurricane off the Virgin Islands, Maurice's ship was swept away and he was lost. 'The sea, to glut itself, swallowed the Prince Maurice, whose fame the mouth of detraction cannot blast, his very enemies bewailing his loss,' lamented the contemporary account of the tragedy. 'Many had more power, few more merit . . . he lived beloved and died bewailed.'

For a long time Elizabeth refused to believe that her son was dead. She clung to the faint hope that he had somehow struggled to shore, and was living, a prisoner, in some exotic land. In the summer of 1654 there came a report that he had been captured by pirates and sold as a slave. Elizabeth was filled with excitement; she quickly got in touch with Rupert, who was staying at Heidelberg, and begged him to set out for Constantinople, to investigate the possibility. Charles Louis sent his mother a somewhat dampening letter, telling her that Rupert 'thinks the way by the Emperor's agent at Constantinople too far about for his liberty (if the news be true)' and advising her that the port of Marseilles would be a better source of information. Elizabeth's reply was still hopeful. 'As for your brother Maurice, I shall shortly know, if it be true that he is there at Algiers and so alive, but I am counselled not to make any great inquiry because, if he be there and known, they may stretch his ransom so high as it will be hard to get it, or else they may for money give him into Cromwell's hands, wherefore Rupert must be very careful that it be not too much openly done.' Cruelly for the bereaved mother, rumours that Prince Maurice was alive persisted for years after his disappearance. To the end of her life Elizabeth never knew for certain what had become of the son she had borne amid the dangers of her flight from Prague.

Of Charles Louis and his affairs she knew all too much. 'I have a son and another a daughter,' she had once written, in hopes that a match might be made between her first-born and the only child of the Swedish champion, Gustavus Adolphus. Long after the scheme had come to nothing, she continued to take a lively interest in Queen Christina; she saw her in person during a visit to Flanders and reported, 'I saw the Queen of Sweden at the play, she is extravagant in her fashion and apparel, but she has a good well-favoured face and a mild countenance. One of the players who knew me told her who I was, but she made no show of it.' If Charles Louis had married Queen Christina of Sweden his domestic life could hardly have been more turbulent than it was with his bride of the house of Hesse. Sophie's original prognosis, that in spite of their complaints about one another the electoral couple seemed very much in love and likely to remain so, proved sadly wrong. Charles Louis displayed a neurotic jealousy about his wife, and she amply returned the compliment, even going so far as to resent his intimacy with Sophie. 'She tried to forbid the Elector's visits to my rooms, but this only made him more determined to come nearly every evening attended by his whole court, at which the anger of the Electress knew no bounds,' Sophie later recalled. It was not to be wondered at that Elizabeth's youngest daughter found life at Heidelberg irksome, and heartily wished by some marriage to escape the difficulties of the situation.

Elizabeth was at first disposed to take her son's part, but when he publicly took a mistress she was deeply upset. 'Truly I will deal plainly with you,' she wrote to him, in 1658, 'your open keeping that wench doth you no small dishonour to all persons of all conditions.' His 'domestic brouilleries' troubled her very much; she was constantly trying to exert her scanty influence to persuade him to be reconciled with his wife, of whom she wrote, 'I confess I never heard any other ill of her but of her choleric unequal humours.' Charles Louis repudiated his electress despite all Elizabeth's efforts to bring them together. Having been so devoted a wife herself, she found it hard to understand her son's marital discord, and could only remind him of his duty. 'If everybody could quit their husbands and wives for their ill humours, there would be no small disorder in the world,' she wrote, 'it is against both God's law and man's law.' She begged him at least to keep up an outward show of respectability. Nothing would satisfy Charles Louis, however, but ʼhe repudiation of his wife and a morganatic marriage with his mistress, Louise von Degenfeld. 'I will not dispute with you the case, though I am not of your mind,' Elizabeth told him, 'having too well read the Scriptures to be of it, besides heard and read few examples of people of your condition have done as you do, so openly to avouch sin.' It was all very distressing for the morally upright and conventional Queen of Bohemia, and it was particularly unhandsome of Charles Louis to reproach her, as he did in February 1661, a year before her death, with the words, 'As for the accidents fallen out in my domestic affairs, it is likely they had not happened if your Majesty had been present.'

The last of Elizabeth's daughters to leave home was the Princess Louise. At the age of thirty-six she was still unmarried, and seemed likely to remain so. She had somewhat boyish good looks; her mother once remarked that when play-acting in men's clothes she could have been mistaken for Rupert. Her departure from The Hague was characteristically unconventional – she simply disappeared one day in December 1657, taking no attendant with her and leaving no hint as to her destination. The note which she left for her horrified mother merely informed her that she had decided to change her religion and enter a Catholic convent.

It turned out that a great friend of Elizabeth's, the Catholic Princess of Zollern, had aided and abetted Louise in her scheme. To make matters worse, this false friend then proceeded to spread cruel rumours about the spinster princess, whispering that she was pregnant. Elizabeth gave a typically robust response to this woman's calumny. 'I need not take the pains to render her infamous,' she wrote, 'she has done it sufficiently herself to all the world by her base mesdisance of Louise, for true or false all the world condemns her for it, either for her betraying the trust of her friend that trusted her, or for basely belying her, which I am confident Louise will prove, for all those that did see her in the monastery do testify she was very free from being with child.' All the family rallied round in the crisis. Young Charles II, the Duke of York and their sister the Princess of Orange went to see Louise in her convent at Antwerp; Elizabeth commented that they did her wayward daughter too much honour, but that their visit would serve the excellent purpose of quelling the rumours of her immorality. King Charles and his sister took Louise to task for her behaviour in leaving her mother so abruptly; she answered, Elizabeth reported, 'that she was very well satisfied with her change, but very sorry that she had displeased me'. Prince Edward was naturally delighted by his sister's conversion. She had confided her intentions to him before she left The Hague, and he gave her encouragement and support. When she left Antwerp for France, Edward fetched her from Rouen and took her to the nunnery at Chaillot; there she was visited by Henrietta Maria and the King of France. 'They are very civil to her,' Elizabeth reported to Rupert, on 29 April 1658. 'The Queen wrote to me that she will have a care of her as of her own daughter, and begs her pardon.' It must have rankled with Elizabeth that her little French sister-in-law should have had the satisfaction of seeing one of her daughters become a Catholic, but she answered her 'as handsomely as I could'. Louise eventually rose to become Abbess of Maubuisson, but she never lost her good humour and her unconventional ways. Later in her long life she was often visited by her niece Elizabeth Charlotte, Duchess of Orleans, Charles Louis's daughter; the Duchess wrote of her as being playful and amusing, and reported that Louise once told her she was happy to get up in the middle of the night to go to church, since her painter's eye appreciated the effects of darkness and shadow. 'She could turn everything in this way so that it should not seem dull.' When she eventually died, in 1709, the accession of Sophie's son George to the throne of England was only five years away.

Elizabeth's youngest daughter had always been greatly concerned with the question of her own marriage prospects. There was a moment when it seemed possible that she might herself become Queen of England; she and her cousin Charles II were close in age, and while the young Stuart exile was at The Hague they became good friends. 'He and I had always been on the best of terms, as cousins and friends, and he had shown a liking for me with which I was much gratified,' Sophie recalled in later life. Though flattered by Charles's interest, she was extremely annoyed by the manner in which he expressed it; the clumsy boy told her, among other things, that she was handsomer than his mistress, Lucy Walter. 'I was highly offended,' Sophie remembered, but her match-making mother took the remark in the spirit in which it was clearly intended, and was cross with her daughter for refusing to take a walk with the king on the following evening. Sophie made the unromantic excuse that she had a corn on her foot, and stayed at home. 'My real reason', she confessed, 'was to avoid the King, having sense enough to know that the marriages of great kings are not made up by such means.'

The princess's subsequent suitors included the emperor's son and the King of Sweden's brother, but at the age of twenty-seven she was still unmarried. Thus it was that when Duke George William of Brunswick-Lüneburg made a formal request for her hand she wasted no time in pretending confusion. 'My answer was not that of a heroine of romance, for I unhesitatingly said yes.' Charles Louis, for his part, did not wait to be asked twice, and the marriage contract was quickly drawn up and signed by all the parties concerned. Later, however, on holiday in Italy, the prospective bridegroom began to regret his decision. Plunged in the dissipations of Venice, he found the idea of marriage, even to the lively and attractive Sophie, increasingly irksome. He came to a startling decision. His youngest brother, Duke Ernest Augustus, should marry the princess instead, 'and receive the family estates, he proposing to retain for himself only a liberal income sufficient for his private expenses'. Furthermore, George William undertook to sign a contract guaranteeing that he would never marry. Charles Louis was furious at the proposal, but Sophie was not displeased. When she met Ernest Augustus at Heidelberg some time before she had thought him the handsomest of the three brothers, and she had enjoyed playing the guitar and dancing with him. There had been the faintest suggestion of a romance; the young duke had offered to send her some of Corbetti's guitar music,

and the princess had felt herself obliged to break off the correspondence which ensued for fear that 'the world might call my friendship
for him by a tenderer name'. She was perfectly willing to marry him
now, saying bluntly, 'A good establishment was all I cared for.'

To Elizabeth's annoyance, the exchange of one proposed son-in-
law for another was arranged without any reference to her. 'I will
not dissemble with you that I wonder you did not let me know of
the change of Sophie's marriage,' she wrote huffily to Charles Louis.
'Since neither my opinion nor consent hath been asked, I have no
more to say, but wish that it may prove for Sophie's content and
happiness.' She did, however, mention that she had a great esteem
for the new bridegroom. No doubt she privately agreed with Charles
Louis when he observed that their family was in no position to be
over-particular.

Sophie was married in great style in the autumn of 1658. She was
dressed in a gown of silver brocade, with a great diamond tiara, and
as her mother had done nearly half a century before, she left her hair
flowing loose in token of virginity. The marriage which had begun
so unconventionally with a substitute bridegroom turned into a love-
match, and Sophie and Ernest Augustus of Brunswick found great
happiness together.

In June 1660 their first child was born. It was a boy. On 14 June
Elizabeth wrote matter-of-factly to Charles Louis, 'I am sure you
know before this that your sister was delivered of a son.' Neither she
nor anyone else could have foreseen that this baby, born in the year
of the Stuart Restoration, was to be the first Hanoverian King of
England.

CHAPTER EIGHT

Eclipse and Glory

'A very debonair, but plain lady' was Samuel Pepys's verdict on the fifty-four-year-old Winter Queen when he saw her in 1660. Elizabeth Stuart's legendary beauty had faded with age and misfortune; her famous golden hair had darkened, thirteen pregnancies had taken their toll of her figure, and the jewels that might have lent a lustre to her looks had long ago been pawned. Only her spirit and charm remained, to give a London diarist with a weakness for actresses the lasting impression of a debonair royal lady.

It was, as she had once written, in spite of fortune that Elizabeth of Bohemia had retained her gallant attitude to life. Hers had been a story of unremitting tragedy and hardship. 'My poor servants are almost starved for lack of board wages, some days I have not turf, sometimes candles nor drink,' she reproached Charles Louis in 1654. 'You may see how melancholic a life I lead and all wonder you do no more for me, who though most miserable and unfortunate am still Your most affectionate mother.' The ungenerous behaviour of her eldest son was not the least of the disappointments she had endured.

The painful discussion of where she was to spend her last years continued to vex her. She told Charles Louis that she was quite willing to live in one of her former dower towns, such as Frankenthal, but this, as he told her, was impossible; 'For no preparation would have made that fit for your living in it, but a whole new building.' He was determined that his mother should come and live under his roof, where he could curb her expenditure, and eventually Elizabeth gave way. 'Winter will hinder my journey, but if you will help me out till the spring, I will make myself ready, God willing, to go, for truly I have done nothing to hinder my going,' she wrote pathetically in October 1654. She was convinced that two households could not live happily together in one establishment. Charles Louis did his best to allay her fears, agreeing to her provisos about the arrangement of her apartments in the castle and assuring her that they would all live as one family. Though Elizabeth loyally protested that she still loved him, her eldest son had long since forfeited her respect and affection, and the prospect of living with him and enduring his domestic disputes depressed her. She who had once reigned at Heidelberg as the gay and beautiful Electress Palatine had no desire at all to return there as a burdensome dowager.

As it turned out, her enormous debts made it impossible for her to leave The Hague. Charles Louis chose to regard this as an excuse. 'As for the creditors, if your Majesty had shown any real desire to come away, they might have been dealt withal,' he told her coldly. In a subsequent letter he added, 'It is believed that if your Majesty had showed the States any earnest intention to come hither, they would have taken some order to have appeased your creditors.' As it was, Elizabeth stayed on at The Hague, constantly appealing to her son for funds. On more than one occasion she had to implore him to redeem precious items of jewellery from pawn; once it was a chain of knots of diamonds that had belonged to her godmother Queen Elizabeth I, and another time 'a great table diamond' that had been Prince Henry's. She attached great sentimental value to such objects; family ties were of the utmost importance to Elizabeth in her old age.

She remained unashamedly partisan in her affections. 'I am of that nature, that whosoever shows kindness to me, I do the like to them and more if it be in my power,' she once wrote, somewhat pointedly, to Charles Louis. Her loyalty to the House of Stuart was intense. Towards the children of her martyred brother Charles I she showed great kindness. She got on well with the eldest boy,

Charles II, and wrote him entertaining letters about the more amusing goings-on at The Hague, but her special favourite was James, the Duke of York. She nicknamed him, obscurely, her 'dear godson Tint'. Unlike his swarthy, French-faced elder brother, James had the light Stuart colouring; perhaps Elizabeth saw in him some resemblance to her adored Prince Henry. She also took a keen interest in the upbringing and education of the youngest boy, Henry, Duke of Gloucester. In 1650 there had been talk of sending him out of England to be brought up by Parliament's friend Charles Louis; 'I conjure you as you love me and mine to accept him upon any conditions,' Elizabeth had written urgently to her son. 'For God's sake make no scruple in receiving him so he be out of those devils' hands.' In September 1655 she was writing fondly of the plan to appoint Sir Charles Cottrell as governor to the boy; he was to be known as his adviser, she wrote, 'for my little gentleman loves not to hear of a governor's name, though he be of a very good nature and not wilful.'

In the boys' sister, Mary, Princess of Orange, Elizabeth had a close friend. Since the time when she had arrived at The Hague as a child-bride, in the care of Henrietta Maria, Elizabeth had watched over her like a mother, and her letters were full of references to her 'dear niece'. Mary, too, had known tragedy : her husband had died young of smallpox, leaving her to bring up his posthumous son on her own. Unlike the resilient Winter Queen, Mary was inclined to be fretful and hypochondriacal, but Elizabeth loved her loyally and took a great pride in her little boy, William. Like many only children he was precocious; 'you cannot imagine the wit that he has, it is not a wit of child,' Elizabeth told Charles Louis. 'He is a very extraordinary child and very good natured.' Her judgement was not borne out by history. As William III of England, husband of James II's daughter Queen Mary, William of Orange was not to be distinguished for either wit or good nature.

When Sophie came to stay with her mother towards the end of 1659 she brought with her a little newcomer – Elizabeth Charlotte, the Elector Palatine's daughter. Elizabeth, who had been a distant mother to most of her own children, was enchanted with her grand-child. 'She is very pretty and you may believe it since I am taken with her, for you know I care not much for children,' she wrote to Charles Louis on 17 November. 'All the Hague is in love with her.' From then on her letters were full of 'Liselotte' and her doings. 'She is a very good child and not troublesome; you may believe me when I commend a child, she being one of the few I like,' wrote the adoring grandmother. 'She is very good-natured and learns very well, she will dance extreme well.' The subject of Liselotte's dancing-lessons occupied a good deal of Elizabeth's attention, and it was with great satisfaction that she reported, on 12 January 1660, that the little girl 'doth already dance the sarabande with the castanets as well as can be'. Her French was also progressing well, and she was bribed to work hard with promises of presents. There was a sad moment when Sophie said, in English, that Liselotte's brother was the better-looking of the two children, 'which she understood and many a tear was shed for it', but Elizabeth quickly announced that she preferred Liselotte's face, 'which much joyed her'. The Winter Queen had her grand-daughter's portrait painted with Celadon, 'the prettiest beagle that ever was seen', and the finished product was sent to Charles Louis, so that he might see 'both my favourites together'. Many years later, as the wife of the odious Philip, Duke of Orleans, and sister-in-law of Louis XIV, Liselotte was to record her verdict on the grandmother who had indulged her. 'Historians often tell lies,' she wrote. 'They tell a story about my grandfather, the King of Bohemia, to the effect that my grandmother, the Queen of Bohemia, inspired by ambition, never gave her husband a moment's peace until he was declared King. There is not a single word of truth in that. The Queen used to think of nothing but seeing comedies and ballets and reading romances.' It was obvious that Liselotte had seen only one side of her grandmother: though Elizabeth had certainly not tormented Frederick into accepting the Bohemian crown, she was far from the ineffectual creature of Liselotte's childhood impression.

The death of Oliver Cromwell in 1658 had given new hope to the Stuarts and their adherents. Elizabeth, to whom England's Protector was the Beast from the Book of Revelations, was overjoyed. 'I fear he is not much at his ease where he now is,' she wrote with evident satisfaction. She observed cautiously to Charles Louis, 'Since Cromwell's death there is no change but it is too soon to look for it.' During the next two years she watched closely for signs of change in England.

It came at last in the spring of 1660. For weeks Elizabeth's letters were full of the activities of General Monck and the hopes of the king's return; phrases such as 'All goes right for the king'; 'Nobody doth doubt but all will be very shortly well' and 'All goes as well as can be in England' revealed her mounting excitement. On 17 May she had great news for Charles Louis : Parliament had voted for the restoration of King Charles II. He was expected at The Hague within a matter of days, to embark for England. He had left his country as a fugitive; now he was to return in triumph, to enjoy his own again. In the peaceful Dutch town which had been Elizabeth's home for forty years all was celebration and festivity. 'There is no other news here but all are overjoyed at the news of England, it is not to be believed how all from the highest to the lowest are overjoyed,' Elizabeth wrote ecstatically.

The charming young King of England was received with great joy and affection by the States-General. It was a supremely happy time for the exiled and impoverished Winter Queen; she was given the place of honour on the king's right hand at banquets, and a stream of English visitors came to pay their respects to her, Mr Samuel Pepys of London among them. The king treated her 'more like a mother than an aunt', to her great satisfaction, and she found him 'the civilest person that can be'. He seemed very conscious of the debt which the House of Stuart owed to her son Prince Rupert, and asked her to write and invite him to stay with him in England, where he would be very welcome. Characteristically, Charles Louis provided the only discordant note amidst the general happiness; he wrote Elizabeth a carping letter, complaining of his newly restored cousin's unkindness in not visiting him at Heidelberg. Elizabeth indignantly rebuked him. 'It was rather your unkindness to him,' she told him, 'he easily saw you had no mind to see him there.' She added pointedly, 'I can assure you all here from the highest to the lowest are very much satisfied with his civilities.'

Charles Louis's disagreeable behaviour apart, Elizabeth had every reason to be happy at this time. Charles II gave her his personal undertaking that Parliament would pay off her debts, and to her delight everyone she met seemed most anxious that she should go over to England. She was very tempted by the idea, far more than she had been by the prospect of living out her remaining days at Heidelberg. 'I may come into England,' she told her eldest son casually. King Charles affectionately made her promise to go over as soon as he sent for her, 'which I confess I am very willing to do', she wrote. She added somewhat defensively, 'It is not strange that I should be glad to see my own country, having been so long out of it, and to be amongst those of my blood to whom I have had so much obligation.'

Late in May King Charles embarked for England. He sailed in the great ship the *Naseby*, now tactfully renamed the *Royal Charles*. The crowds who flocked to see him depart were so huge that the royal party became separated; Elizabeth and the young king were rowed out alone, in one of the ship's boats, to where the royal barge was waiting to take them on board. The Princess of Orange and the king's brothers met up with them there, having lost them earlier in the crush of people. It was a deeply moving occasion for the sister of the martyred Charles I. As soon as they had him in, the sailors roared out, 'We have him, we have him, God bless King Charles!' To Elizabeth, the Restoration was a triumphant proof of divine justice. 'God will not always prosper ill actions, as you see by the King's restoring and his rebels' pulling down,' she wrote confidently.

1660 was a momentous year for the Stuarts, but it brought them misfortunes as well as joys. In the autumn the king's youngest brother, Henry, Duke of Gloucester, died of smallpox. The death of children was nothing new to Elizabeth, but she was deeply saddened by the loss of this nephew, whom, she told Charles Louis, she had loved as her own child. 'I confess his death has afflicted me very much, he had a great respect and kindness for me, and I loved him extremely,' she wrote.

If the death of the Duke of Gloucester was 'a great loss to our House', so, in her opinion, was the marriage of the Duke of York. 'Nan Hyde, the Chancellor's daughter', was well-known to her; daughter of the future Lord Clarendon, and maid of honour to the Princess of Orange, Anne was a lively, cheerful young woman with a talent for acting. Elizabeth's letters mentioned her more than once, at parties, looking very handsome in fancy dress; on one occasion she was a shepherdess, another time a gipsy's wife. Towards the end of 1660, however, some agitated references to 'Hyde' began to appear in Elizabeth's correspondence. She seemed very anxious to refute rumours that young James, the Duke of York, had contracted a secret marriage with the maid of honour. It was evident that she was his mistress, and pregnant, but that so ill-matched a marriage could have taken place was out of the question – 'that neither is or will ever be', Elizabeth wrote decisively. A few weeks later she produced triumphant proof that no such wedding had taken place. It appeared that Mistress Hyde had gone to the physician, Dr Rumph, with a story about having eaten too much fish during Lent, and asked him 'to give her physic to carry all away'. The doctor proceeded to administer 'good strong purges and vomits', and bled her in the foot, but suddenly he noticed her condition, and stopped the treatment with haste. 'If it had been a marriage she would not have sought to destroy the child, and this is most true,' Elizabeth concluded.

But whatever Anne's reasons for wishing to abort the duke's child, it turned out that she was indeed his legal wife, and there was noth-ing his horrified relations could do to alter the fact. 'I have already written to you concerning my Godson's marriage, which afflicts all his kindred and doth himself no small wrong,' the Winter Queen wrote to Charles Louis. She was particularly perturbed by the effect which this 'base marriage' might be having on the spirits of her beloved niece, the Princess of Orange, who was ill with the smallpox.

The princess had gone to England at the time of Gloucester's death. She was sad to leave her only child, young William, who was studying at Leiden, but she longed to see her brothers and England again. Her happiness at returning to the country of her birth was destined to be short-lived however. 'My niece has gotten the smallpox, which puts me in great pain for her, since her Brother died of it,' Elizabeth wrote anxiously, late in December. Her fears were all too well-founded. Mary died on Christmas Eve. 'As soon as she fell sick, she said she should die, but was not at all afraid of it and rather seemed willing to die,' Elizabeth was informed. She had been one of the less popular Stuarts; haughty in public and fretful in private, she was not greatly missed either at The Hague or in England. Elizabeth was one of the few who had sincerely loved her, and she was deeply grieved by her death. 'I am so sad, I fear I write nonsense,' she told Charles Louis at the end of the letter in which she had recounted the details of her niece's end. In a subsequent letter she wrote touchingly, 'I shall never forget her memory; we lived almost twenty years together and always loved one another.' On her deathbed Mary, who 'made a very godly end', asked her brother King Charles to take her orphaned son into his protection; when the news reached Elizabeth her first thought was for the ten-year-old boy, and she made the journey out to Leiden to comfort him.

With Mary gone for ever, The Hague became increasingly irksome as a place of residence for the sociable Winter Queen. England was once more the Promised Land, and the court at Whitehall was, by all reports, as gay as it had been in her girlhood. She longed to return to London, to take her place as the king's honoured aunt. The troublesome question of her going to live at Heidelberg with Charles Louis continued to be a source of vexation : she wanted to have her dower house at Frankenthal put in order for her, he insisted that he could not afford to maintain two households, and so the wrangling went on. 'There are such accidents fallen out in your domestic affairs that I thank God I am not there,' Elizabeth told her eldest son sharply early in 1661, but two months later she assured him that she was certainly not refusing to go to Germany, she had simply not made up her mind. The truth was that the idea of going to England was now uppermost in her thoughts.

'I cannot yet tell you when I shall go, I am confident it will be this summer, you shall know it when I know it,' she wrote to Charles Louis in the spring. At the time of his departure King Charles had issued a warm invitation to his aunt to visit him, but though she waited expectantly the weeks passed with no further word on the subject. His silence could be attributed to his preoccupation with the forthcoming coronation; once that was over Elizabeth decided to take matters into her own hands. 'Now I hear that the coronation is so happily passed, I have no more patience to stay here, but am resolved to go myself to congratulate that happy action,' she wrote to a friend. She explained, 'I would not do it before, not to give the King too much trouble at once, except he had commanded me to go, and now I assure you I shall give very little trouble, for I bring with me not above 26 or 27 persons.' The drift of her reasoning was clear; as long as she was no burden to her nephew Charles II, he surely could have no objection to her presence in his country. 'I go with a resolution to put myself wholly into his hands, and obey him in all things, and trouble him for nobody,' she wrote. The question of where she would stay in London was taken care of; the ever-devoted Lord Craven had put his town house in Drury Lane at her disposal. Invited or not, she was at last bound for England.

She apparently did not intend her stay there to be permanent. According to Louis XIV's ambassador at The Hague, De Thou, she talked of returning to The Hague, 'but I doubt whether the King her nephew will permit her to do so', De Thou commented. He thought that such a gracious and charming member of the English royal family would be so popular in her own country that her presence there would be good for the Stuarts' prestige. As evidence of her ability to make herself generally beloved, he quoted the fact that the local Dutch tradesmen to whom she owed more than two hundred thousand crowns were prepared to let her go without a murmur, not doubting that she would honour her debts as soon as she possibly could.

The French ambassador commented that the Queen of Bohemia still enjoyed excellent health both of body and mind, even though she was 'more than a sexagenarian in age'. Before she set out for England, however, Elizabeth thought it prudent to make her will. She had once declared her intention of leaving all her valuables away from the self-seeking Charles Louis, and that was what she proceeded to do. 'Dear Rupert' was now the favoured child, and to him she left most of her scanty possessions, dividing up her few remaining jewels among the others.

Farewells were exchanged, visits paid, she took leave of her Dutch hosts and accepted the loan of the French ambassador's coach; everything was in readiness when the blow fell. The captain of a little English frigate arrived in haste, bearing an official letter. The King of England, busy with his own affairs and amusements, was not ready to receive her. The Winter Queen was requested to postpone her journey until Charles II should choose to invite her. It was a sad moment for the ageing Elizabeth Stuart.

She was now in a singularly embarrassing situation. Not only were her bags packed and her affairs settled in anticipation of the voyage, she had 'taken farewell of all public and private', and she now had no 'handsome excuse to stay'. If it became generally known that the king had asked her not to come after all, she wrote, 'it would be taken as disaffection to her, which would make her despised in all places'. To Prince Rupert, who had sent her a letter 'to the same purport' as the king's, telling her she must put off her visit, she outlined her predicament. 'I cannot now stay here,' she told him flatly. She made up her mind. She would go to England as planned, see the king, and 'stay no longer than he shall think fit'. It was not the way the former darling of the English nation had thought to return home, but, she wrote, 'I go with a resolution to suffer all things constantly, I thank God he has given me courage.'

When Elizabeth had made the journey down the Thames as a young bride bound for her new country in the spring of 1613, vast crowds had thronged the river-bank. While the people waved and cheered, the great guns had boomed out their loyal salutes to the beautiful and beloved princess who was leaving home. Now, nearly half a century later, she returned almost unnoticed. She came up the river after dark, to hide the absence of a royal welcome. Memories of times past must have crowded into Elizabeth's mind as she came gliding up the Thames, but Restoration London went about its night-time business unmoved by the return of a faded Jacobean beauty.

It was openly said that the Winter Queen had come to England against the wishes of the king, and that her visit would not be a long one. The fact that she was not given apartments at court was cited as evidence of Charles's disinclination to entertain her. Lord Craven, however, proved a kind friend and a generous host, and at his house in fashionable Drury Lane Elizabeth was lodged in comfort. The rumours which grew up in later years, that the Winter Queen finally married William Craven, were entirely unfounded. The daughter of James I had the strictest notions of social distinctions, as was demonstrated by her outrage at the 'base marriage' of James the Duke of York with Anne Hyde, the Chancellor's daughter, and the devoted widow of the King of Bohemia would not have married the *nouveau riche* son of a Lord Mayor of London. There is another certainty : since Elizabeth would never have made a marriage which she considered in any way dishonourable, any marriage which she did make would have been openly acknowledged. Directness and honesty were among her most striking characteristics throughout her life. William Craven was no more to her than a cherished friend and devoted admirer.

At the time of Elizabeth's arrival in London the royal family were in mourning for the death of a baby, the little Duke of Cambridge, the son whom the Duke of York and Anne Hyde had conceived before their clandestine marriage. It was another link in the strange chain of events which was eventually to bring Elizabeth's grandson to the throne of England. The death of an infant, even one so close to the crown, could not long dampen the spirits of the Stuart court, however, and the customary round of gaieties was soon resumed. 'All goes very well here, the Duchess of York is gone to drink Tunbridge waters, having drunk Barnet waters before,' Elizabeth reported in July.

Whatever King Charles's initial reaction to his aunt's defiance of his wishes might have been, he was by temperament far too easy-going to bear any grudge for her behaviour, and although he did not offer her lodgings at Whitehall, he was happy to act as her escort in public. 'Yesterday the King and I were at Kensington, feasted by the Duke of Ormond,' Elizabeth wrote happily, 'there was very good company.' She went on with great satisfaction: 'Every week I march to one place or other with the King.' It was generally agreed that the Queen of Bohemia was, despite her age and circumstances, a lady of great charm and liveliness, and the genial Charles Stuart probably enjoyed her company. Elizabeth's pleasure at finding herself once more in English society shone out of her letters, as she passed on the news and gossip of London to Charles Louis.

On 2 July King Charles accompanied his aunt to a performance of the *Siege of Rhodes*, by Sir William Davenant – 'Davenant's opera, as he calls it', Elizabeth wrote fondly. Samuel Pepys was in the audience that evening, and found it 'very fine and magnificent and well-acted, all but the Eunuch', but Elizabeth's enjoyment of the play was marred by some distressing news which had arrived just before the king came to collect her.

Though she had come to England fully intending to stay only a short while before returning to The Hague, she had now made up her mind to settle in London. She had therefore sent for her remaining furniture and belongings from her former homes, the Wassanaer Hof and Rhenen. Then, as she was dressed and ready for the theatre, word arrived from one of her servants, Michel, that the Elector Palatine's agent at The Hague had ordered all her 'stuff' to be held up. The man had gone so far as to try to 'procure my creditors to arrest my goods' as Elizabeth indignantly reported. She did her best to exonerate her son from blame; 'I neither can nor do believe he did this by your order,' she told Charles Louis. She was so full of wrath at the news that she poured it all out to King Charles when he appeared, and he politely declared that he was 'much surprised at it'.

As Elizabeth no doubt suspected, despite her protestations to the contrary, Charles Louis was indeed responsible for the interference

with his mother's goods. He told her that he had certainly not tried
to stir up her creditors; he had merely stayed the furniture until he
had satisfied himself that nothing which was rightfully his was being
sent away. Elizabeth was furious. 'If I had as much means to buy
hangings as my Lord Craven has, I should not have been so rigorous
as to take what is my right,' she told him haughtily. 'Though you
cannot afford me a house, you need not grudge me the little I have
from your house, which I take not as reprisals but my right.' A
considerable degree of acrimony developed in their letters. 'I can
easily perceive how willing your Majesty is the world should perceive,
upon any occasion, that you find fault with me,' Charles Louis wrote.
He had heard that his mother had publicly criticized him, in front
of the Brandenburg ambassador, 'which, though I had committed a
much greater fault, you would not have done, if you were not willing
to have myself and all the world take notice of your constant settled
displeasure against me, as you have also showed in many other
occasions'. Elizabeth indignantly denied having spoken ill of him to
anyone, saying it was 'a false lie'. She added with asperity, 'I assure
you none is more sorry than I am when I hear people censure you
for your actions, I assure you, I do not do it before folks, but thoughts
are free.' The son on whom she had lavished her tenderest maternal
love had grown up to be a sad disappointment to her in her old age.
Nevertheless, she loyally kept up appearances. 'Farewell, God bless
you and make you see the truth of all things, then you will know
I am still your true good Mother,' she ended one of her last letters
to him.

The fame and popularity of the Winter Queen were long past their
height by the time she returned to London in 1661. Yet even in her
eclipse, at the age of sixty-four, she had the power to charm those
who met her. The Genoese ambassador described how he paid a call
on her one autumn evening, and was most graciously received, first
by Lord Craven, and then by Elizabeth herself, who showed great
pleasure at his visit and conversed with him for a long time about
politics and other topics. The ambassador came away deeply impressed with her. 'This princess has learned from nature, and

continued through the changes of her fortune, an incomparable goodness,' he wrote. 'Now she is restored to some authority, and thus is heightened the lustre of that affable manner with which she wonderfully conciliates the esteem and love of the court.' The tragedies and misfortunes of Elizabeth's life were past, and though her stay in Restoration England was to be short it was happy. As the aunt of the king, and the mother of the Cavaliers' hero Prince Rupert, she enjoyed considerable social status, and for the first time in many years she was not penniless, as Charles II had settled £1,000 a month on her for life. 'I am delighted that your Majesty has so much cause to be pleased with the King your nephew,' Sophie wrote from Hanover, in August.

Elizabeth's youngest daughter made it plain that she envied her mother's good fortune at living in fashionable London. No doubt she, Sophie, must seem 'very homely' compared to the beautiful ladies of Charles II's court, she wrote. 'There will no doubt be a great deal of magnificence in London when the beautiful Infanta arrives,' she observed wistfully. The sophistication of her new surroundings was not wasted on Elizabeth, even though she was now a grandmother of sixty-five; she wrote to Edward in Paris, commissioning him to find her the latest trimmings for her clothes, as well as some pretty accessories, such as *étui* cases and little scissors. She included a request for one of the popular romances, *Pharamond*. Edward, who was himself the height of elegance, applied himself to the task with energy, and in his reply to his mother he interspersed the news of the birth of the dauphin – who, it appeared, was 'pale, handsome and large' – with the information that sable muffs were being worn smaller that season.

Elizabeth did not intend to take advantage of Lord Craven's hospitality for longer than was necessary; she wanted to maintain her independence. At the end of January 1662, she removed her little household to Leicester House, in Leicester Fields. She had recently had a bad cold, but she seemed to have recovered, and on 10 January she was well enough to write to Charles Louis. She told him gaily that she had been persuaded by her doctors 'to take physic, to be quite rid of my cold, which I believe you doubt not but I did very unwillingly, and it made me as sick as a dog'. She went on to say that her own favourite cure, blood-letting, had done the most good, 'for now I am very well'.

Ever since her long-ago Scottish childhood, the Winter Queen had thrived on cold, bracing air; 'heat is always more troublesome to me than cold,' she once wrote. This January was unnaturally warm. 'It is so hot weather here as I have felt it colder in May,' she told Charles Louis. The elector observed politely that the coming of spring would no doubt do his mother good, but Elizabeth was not to see another spring. The good health of her youth had deserted her after her husband's death, and she had become prone to chest trouble. Now it returned, with frightening force.

On 10 February she suffered a haemorrhage of the lungs, and her nephews Charles ii and the Duke of York, with the Chancellor, Lord Clarendon, were sent for. She took communion, according to the rites of the Church of England, and when the King of England appeared solicitously at her bedside she was prepared for death. Of all the sons and daughters she had borne, it was the most fitting that Prince Rupert should have been with her during her last hours. His love of England, his courage and his loyalty to the House of Stuart reflected hers, and he had become the dearest of her children. 'I love you ever, my dear Rupert,' she had written tenderly, just before she left The Hague for England.

Elizabeth died on 13 February 1662, within a few hours of the forty-eighth anniversary of her wedding-day. At the fickle, fashionable Restoration court she was not deeply mourned. Lord Leicester commented on the departure of his royal tenant, and regretted the absence of a John Donne to write her an epitaph; Charles ii and her 'dear godson Tint' did not feel it necessary to attend her funeral, which took place four days later.

The ceremony was, however, elaborate and gorgeous, as befitted her status as a Stuart princess. With Prince Rupert as chief mourner, the procession wound its way down the Thames by night, as far as Westminster Bridge. 'This night was buried in Westminster Abbey the Queen of Bohemia, after all her sorrows and afflictions,' wrote John Evelyn in his diary. By the light of wax tapers the coffin was carried into the Henry VII Chapel, and laid to rest, as Elizabeth had wished, beside the body of her beloved brother Henry, among the remains of her royal ancestors. While the burial service was being read there arose a strange discord in the night sky outside; the mourners heard 'such a storm of hail, thunder and lightning, as never was seen the like in any man's memory'. It was a dramatic leave-taking to an eventful life.

The woman whom the Winter King had called his 'soul's star' was in eclipse at the end of her life, yet a glory which no one could have foreseen was to be hers. Though she and her husband had lost their Bohemian throne after only one year, her direct descendants, from her grandson onwards, were to wear the crown of England throughout the succeeding generations; the god-daughter and namesake of Queen Elizabeth I was to be the ancestress of Queen Elizabeth II.

Index

Albert, Archduke, 51
Alonso de Velasco, 28
Amberg, 60, 71
Amsterdam, 51, 95, 101
Anne of Denmark, Queen of
England, 7, 12, 15, 20, 42, 63;
mother of Elizabeth Stuart, 2–4;
Catholic sympathies, 13, 28, 39;
character, 16; Danish family, 21,
26
Ansbach, Margrave of, 71
Antwerp, 139
Apsley, Elizabeth, 63–4
Arbella Stuart, 24
Arundel, Lord, 111–12, 117, 120
Ashby, 7
Ashby St Legers, 14
Austria, 95, 119

Bacharach, 52
Bacon, Sir Francis, 46
Baden-Durlach, Margrave of, 91
Banqueting House, 30, 36, 44, 130
Bavaria, 79, 85
Bavaria, Duke of, see Maximilian
Beaumont, de, 10
Bedford, Lady, 7, 62, 94
Berlin, 84

Bernard, Duke of Saxe-Weimar,
119
Berwick-on-Tweed, 7
Bess of Hardwick, 24
Bethlen Gabor, Prince of Transyl-
vania, 75, 79
Blake, Admiral, 135
Boderie, le Fevre de la, 16
Bohemia, 28, 64–5, 68, 75, 89, 120
Boswell, William, 111, 120–1
Bouillon, Duke de, 24–5, 69–70, 92
Bowes, Robert, 3
'Boy', 120, 122
Brabant, 62
Brandenburg, Margrave of, 52, 85
Breda, 87
Breslau, 84
Bristol, 125, 126
'Britain's Burse', 17
Brunswick, Sophia Hedwig of, 51
Brunswick-Wolfenbüttel, Duke of,
90
Buckingham, Marquis of, 68, 73,
85, 90, 93, 96–100
Bull, Dr John, 12
Burka, Baron, 72

Calvinism, 28, 55, 73, 76, 91

Cambridge, 48
Cambridge, Duke of, 152
Canterbury, 49
Canterbury, Archbishop of, 35, 37, 69
Carleton, Sir Dudley, 63, 87, 93–5
Carlisle, Lord, 102
Catesby, Robert, 13, 14
Catholic League, 69, 91
Catholicism: in Scotland, 4; in England, 13; in Spain, 22, 51; in Central Europe, 55, 64–5, 68–9, 73, 87, 115; *see also* Habsburgs
Caus, Solomon de, 64
Cecil, Robert, 6, 13, 14
Chaillot, 139
Chamberlain, 48, 62
Chapman, George, 45
Charles I, 1, 4, 5, 16, 30, 35, 45, 48–9, 84, 130; as king, 57, 98, 104–5; and marriage, 68, 86, 93, 97, 100, 103; and Elizabeth Stuart's family, 79, 105, 112–17, 124, 126–7, 143
Charles II, 1, 103; and Elizabeth Stuart's family, 131, 134, 139–40, 144, 150, 156; Restoration of, 146; character, 153
Charles Louis, 62, 79, 94, 108, 114; and Elizabeth, 101, 124, 129, 131, 133–4, 136, 138, 142, 149, 153; as heir and Elector Palatine, 109, 117, 119, 124, 129, 140; and England, 112, 114–15, 117, 128; character, 115, 124, 127; and marriage, 121, 132, 137–8
Charlotte, Princess, 101, 104
Charlotte, Elizabeth of Hesse-Cassel 132
Christian IV of Denmark, 15, 26, 99
Christian of Anhalt, 54, 69, 82–3

Christian of Brunswick, 90–2, 95–6, 99, 108
Christina of Sweden, 116, 137
Civil War, 1, 101, 106, 120–2, 136
Clarendon, Lord, 156
Cloister Church of The Hague, 104, 105
'Cockpit', 19, 112
Combe Abbey, 8, 11, 14, 15, 106
Constantinople, 136
Constant Reformation, 135
Conway, Lord, 81–3, 95, 98, 100
Corbetti, 140
Cottrell, Sir Charles, 144
Coventry, 8, 14
Craven, William Lord, 106, 117–18, 133, 150, 152, 155
Cromwell, Oliver, 126, 130, 136
Custrin, 84–5

Daniel, Samuel, 20
Darnley, Lord, 4, 24
Davenant, Sir William, 153
Defenestration of Prague, 65, 72
Delft, 51, 96
Denmark, 99
Descartes, 113, 132
De Thou, 150
Digby, Lord, 89
Dohna, Baron Christopher, 82
Doncaster, Lord, 70, 102
Donne, Dr John, 1, 2, 71, 93
Dudley, Anne, 61

Edgehill, Battle of, 125
Edinburgh, 3, 57, 123
Edmondes, Sir Thomas, 26
Edward, Prince, 98, 112, 119, 127, 130, 132, 139, 155
Elizabeth I, 1, 2, 6, 90
Elizabeth II, 157
Elizabeth of Denmark, 21, 51

Elizabeth of Hungary, 74
Elizabeth Stuart, 7, 11, 32, 36, 38; character, 10, 17, 18, 43, 55, 70–1, 74, 81, 83–4, 95, 111, 114, 126, 142, 152–6; suitors, 10, 16, 17, 21–5; and Henry, Prince of Wales, 12, 15, 18, 34, 39, 143; and religion, 12, 27, 72, 84, 93, 116, 121, 127, 138; popularity, 14, 44, 48, 50–3, 57, 72–3, 77–8, 90, 150; and James I, 15–17, 23, 27, 49, 50, 56–7, 61, 63, 79–80, 87, 89, 95–6; and Frederick V, 26, 31, 33, 43, 48, 52, 64, 66, 69, 80–1, 85, 89, 92, 111; financial position, 27, 47, 51–2, 55–6, 58, 60, 123, 126, 130, 133–5, 142–3, 153; and children, 41–7, 56, 62, 70, 82, 85, 94, 98, 103–5, 109, 111, 113, 119, 145; and Charles Louis, 101, 124, 129, 131, 133–4, 136–8, 142, 149, 153
Elizabeth, Princess, 63, 79, 94, 101, 113, 116, 132–3
Elizabeth Charlotte, Duchess of Orleans, 139, 144
Ernest Augustus, 140–1
Ernest, Count Mansfeld, 91
Essex, Earl of, 102
Essex House, 31
Evelyn, John, 157
Exton Hall, 11

Fabricius, 65
Fawkes, Guy, 13–15
Felton, John, 100
Ferdinand III, 118
Ferdinand of Styria, 65–6, 69, 71, 75, 79, 86, 89
Flanders, 62, 137
Flushing, 49, 50
France, 97, 119

Frankenthal, 52, 93, 106–7, 142
Frankfurt, 66
Frederick IV, 54
Frederick V, Elector Palatine, 25–6, 28, 30, 31, 36, 38, 47, 55; and Henry, Prince of Wales, 15, 31, 35; and James I, 31, 45, 65, 68, 70, 76, 85, 92; popularity in England, 37, 44; and Charles I, 37, 50; and religion, 55–69, 71, 76; health, 58–61, 89, 92, 95, 98, 103, 108; as King of Bohemia, 65–70, 71–3, 81–2; as exile, 83–5, 95, 105, 107–8
Frederick Henry, Prince, 57, 58, 60, 63, 70, 75, 80, 94, 96, 99, 101–2
Frederick Ulrich of Brunswick, 21

Gaulheim, 52
Gelderland, 100
George I, 2, 139, 141
George Frederick, Margrave of Baden-Durlach, 91
George William, Elector of Brandenburg, 84
George William, Duke of Brunswick-Lüneburg, 140
Gonzague, Anne de, 127
Goring, Lord, 111
Gravesend, 16
Greenwich Palace, 16
Greville, Sir Fulke, 14
Grey, Katherine, 24
Grey, Lady Jane, 24
Gunpowder Plot, 13–15
Gustavus Adolphus, King of Sweden, 21, 104–8, 116
Gustavus Adolphus, Prince, 105, 113

Haarlem, 95

Habsburgs, 35, 64, 68–9, 72, 117;
  see also Catholicism
Hague, The, 50, 87–8, 99, 102, 116,
  120, 143, 149
Hamilton, Marquis of, 35, 104, 106
Hampton Court, 10
Hanover, 155
Harington, Lady, 7, 8, 16, 62
Harington, Lord, 11, 14, 15, 17,
  47, 49, 55, 63
Harrison, John, 70
Hatzfeld, Count, 118
Hay, Alison, 11
Hay, Lady Eleanor, 4
Heidelberg, 49, 51, 53, 60, 64, 70,
  79, 91–2, 102, 106–7, 129, 132,
  136, 140, 143, 147
Heilbronn, 58
Henrietta Maria, Queen of
  England, 97, 99, 101, 103, 115,
  121–2, 131, 139, 144
Henrietta Maria, Princess, 99, 113,
  133
Henry IV of France, 10, 22, 54
Henry VII of England, 24
Henry, Duke of Gloucester, 144,
  147
Henry of Nassau, 28, 33; as Prince
  of Orange, 101, 111, 114–15
Henry, Prince of Wales, 13, 15, 22;
  popularity, 3, 9, 19, 34; character,
  4, 5, 10–11, 16, 21, 26, 32–4;
  marriage plans, 16, 22
Herald, Lyon, 3
Hochst, 106
Holbeach, 14
Holland, 50, 91, 121
Holyrood House, 3
Honest Seaman, 135
Hopkins, 14
Hopton, Ralph, 84
Hradschin Palace, 65, 73, 79, 81–2

Hungary, 64
Hussites, 77
Hyde, Anne, 148, 152

India, 77
Infanta of Spain, 68, 93, 96, 97
Isabella of Spain, 51

Jacobean court, 10, 15, 17, 19–20,
  32, 39–40, 45–6, 48
James, Duke of York, 139, 144,
  148, 152, 156
James I of England, 6, 9, 11, 13,
  58, 98; marriage, 3; character, 4,
  6, 12, 16, 45–6, 94; and religion,
  13, 23, 68; and policies, 65–6,
  68, 70, 76, 80, 85–6, 89, 92–5, 97
Jones, Inigo, 12, 20, 30, 45
Jonson, Ben, 12, 17, 18

Kildare, Countess of, 7, 8, 11
King, General, 118
Knot of Fools, 38
Kreuznach, 106

Lake, Sir Thomas, 37
Laud, Archbishop, 112, 117
Leicester, 7
Leicester House, 155
Leicester, Lord, 1, 156
Leiden, 94, 99, 101, 106, 108, 112,
  148
Leopold, Archduke, 120
l'Epinay, Jacques de, 128
Linlithgow, 4
Linlithgow, 1st Earl of, 4, 5
Linlithgow, 2nd Earl of, 5
Linz, 119–22
Lippe, Colonel, 118
'Liselotte', see Elizabeth Charlotte
Livingstone, Lord, 4
Lixheim, 100, 105

Lord High Admiral, 50
Lord Mayor of London, 32
Louis XIII of France, 76, 96
Louis XIV of France, 145
Louis, Prince, 96, 98
Louise Hollandine, Princess, 91, 94, 113, 128, 131, 138–9
Louise Juliana, Electress Palatine, 26, 38, 54, 59, 60, 62, 69, 70, 77, 91, 126
Lower Palatinate, *see* Palatinate
Lutherans, 55, 73, 76, 107
Lutter, Battle of, 99
Lutzen, Battle of, 108

Madagascar, 115
Madrid, 93
Mannheim, 92
Mansfeld, Count, 91, 97–9, 108
Mar, Countess of, 5
Mar, Earl of, 4, 5
Margaret Stuart, 5
Margate, 49, 50
Marseilles, 136
Marston Moor, Battle of, 126
Martinitz, 65
Mary, Princess of Orange, 109, 121, 139, 144, 147–8
Mary, Queen of Scots, 2, 4
Matthias, Emperor of Bohemia, 64–6
Maubuisson, 139
Maurice, Prince, 85, 94, 100, 112, 119; following Rupert as soldier, 114, 116, 120, 122, 125, 130, 134; marriage plans for, 127; death, 135–6
Maurice, Prince of Orange, 50–1, 101; and Elizabeth's family, 21, 58, 69, 87, 94; army of, 87, 90, 103

Maximilian of Bavaria, 55, 66, 69, 79, 118, 120, 129
Mayerne, Dr, 34
Médicis, Marie de, 22, 97
Merry Devil of Edmonton, 38
Middleburgh, 50
Mingolsheim, 91
Moldau, 76
Monck, General, 146
Mondorf, 52
Montrose, James Graham, Marquis of, 131, 132
Moors, 71
Moravia, 84
Much Ado About Nothing, 38
Mühlhausen, 75
Münster, 129

Naseby, 147
Nethersole, Sir Francis, 79, 80, 82, 87, 96
Nevers, Duke de, 127
Newmarket, 48
Northampton, Earl of, 22, 44, 49
Nottingham, 122

Oatlands, 10, 11
Oppenheim, 108
Orange, Princess of, *see* Mary
Ormond, Duke of, 153
Oxford, 48, 130

Palatinate (Upper and Lower), 15, 25, 54, 60, 64, 69–70, 80, 85, 89, 91, 95, 97, 104–7, 118, 129
'Palsgrave', 28, 31, 54; *see also* Frederick V
Paris, 97, 122
Peace of Westphalia, 129
Pepys, Samuel, 114, 142, 146, 153
Percy, Thomas, 13, 14
Pett, Phineas, 20, 21, 49, 50

Pharamond, 155
Philip III of Spain, 25
Philip, Duke of Orleans, 145
Philip, Prince, 100, 119, 128–9
Plessen, de, 94, 107–8
Poland, King of, 116
Portugal, 135
Powick Bridge, Battle of, 122
Prague, 65, 66, 70, 72, 76, 77, 81, 84
Prince Royal, 20, 21, 49
Protestantism, 23, 25, 64, 65, 68, 69, 71, 76, 89, 104, 108; *see also* Calvinism and Lutherans

Raleigh, Sir Walter, 16, 22, 23, 25
Restoration, 1, 146; *see also* Charles II
Rethel, 129
Rheinbeck, 51
Rhenen, 100, 103, 153
Richelieu, Cardinal, 119
Roe, Sir Thomas, 77–8, 89, 91, 94, 98, 102, 105, 110, 114–22, 126
Rohan, Mademoiselle de, 127
Rotterdam, 51, 87
Rouen, 139
Royal Charles, 147
Rumph, Dr, 109, 148
Rupa, Baron, 72
Rupert III, 25
Rupert, Elector Palatine, 74
Rupert, Prince, of the Rhine, 1, 74–5, 82–3, 92, 94, 106, 112–21; in England, 122, 127–8, 135–6, 146, 151, 155–6; religion, 122–3; and Elizabeth, 133–4; *see also* Civil War
Rutland, 11

Sainte Catherine, M. de, 57
St James's Palace, 39, 45, 97

St Vitus, Cathedral of, 73, 75
St Wenceslas, Chapel of, 73
Saxe-Weimar, 119
Schevening, 95
'Schomberg' (Meinhard von Schönberg), 27, 28, 53, 56, 58, 59, 61
Scultetus, 73, 76
Sedan, 92
Seymour, William, 24
Shakespeare, 1
Siege of Rhodes, 153
Siegmund Rakoczy, 133
Silesia, 84
Simmern, House of, 25
Slavata, 65
'Smith, Jack and Tom', 93
Sophia Stuart, 15
Sophia-Hedwig of Brunswick, 51
Sophie, Princess, 94, 103, 113, 121–2, 130–3, 137, 139–41, 144, 155
Spain, 22, 69, 79, 85–7, 91, 93, 95–6, 97–8, 101, 104, 135
Spanish Netherlands, 51, 79
Spinola, Ambrogio, 79, 80, 92
Star Park, Prague, 72, 82
Stirling, 4
Strafford, Lord, 121
Swallow, 135
Sweden, 99
Sweden, King of, *see* Gustavus Adolphus
Sweden, Queen of, 106

Tagus, 135
Tempest, The, 38
Theobalds, 34, 98
Thirty Years' War, 1, 75, 76, 81, 98, 129
Thurn, Count, 65
Tilly, Count, 82, 91, 99

Trémoille, Duchess Charlotte de la, 57, 84

Union of German Protestant Princes, 28, 50, 54, 58, 69, 76, 79, 80, 99
Upper Palatinate, *see* Palatinate
Utrecht, 51, 100

Van der Myle, Madam, 88
Van Dyck, 122
Vane, Sir Henry, 108–9
Venice, 140
Vere, Sir Horace, 76, 93
Victor Amadeus of Savoy, 22
Vienna, 117
Villiers, Sir Edward, 85–7
Virgin Islands, 136
Vladislav of Poland, 116
Vlotho, 118
von Degenfeld, Louise, 138

Walden, Lord Howard de, 22
Waldsassen, 72
Walter, Lucy, 140

Wassenaer Hof, 88, 153
West India Company, 101
Westminster Abbey, 1, 156
Weston, 81, 83
Whitehall Palace, 19, 41, 149
William III, 144, 148
William of Orange, 121
William the Silent, 54, 132
Windsor, 8, 10
Winter, Thomas, 13
Winwood, Sir Ralph, 51, 59
Wittelsbach, House of, 25
Woolwich, 20
Worms, 55
Wotton, Sir Henry, 61, 78
Württemberg, Duke of, 28, 56

York, 7
York, James, Duke of, 139, 144, 148, 152, 156

Zollern, Princess of, 138
Zuniga, Pedro de, 26
Zweibrücken, Duke of, 62

257